Table of Contents

Preface

Target Audience

This book is for developers who are currently using Microsoft ASP.NET and MVC to create websites, and who are interested in creating websites that play nicely with mobile devices or want to update their existing site. If that's you, I'm assuming that you already have a working knowledge of MVC, so this book will not give you introductory lessons of what MVC is or tell you how to use it. It's designed to be a quick read for developers and to help them understand the concepts they need to know to improve their websites when it comes to dealing with mobile devices.

Tools Needed

In order to be able to follow along with all of the examples in this book, you will need the following:

- Microsoft Visual Studio 2010 or Visual Studio 2012

- MVC 4 (Although most of this book targets MVC 4, Chapter 11 addresses how you can implement these concepts in MVC 3). This book is based on the MVC 4 RTM version.

If you have something less than this list, you may or may not be able to run all of the examples.

Formatting

Throughout the book, I have used several formatting conventions.

Code Blocks

```
protected void Application_Start()
```

Personal Comments

This is a comment related to the current section.

Using Code Examples

The sample projects are available at
https://bitbucket.org/syncfusion/mobilemvc-succinctly.

This book is designed to help you learn the techniques quickly and get your job done, so you are free to use the code in this book for your programs or documentation. You do not need to contact the author for permission unless you are reproducing major portions of the code or writing a program based on one of the example projects. Answering a question by citing this book and quoting examples does not require permission.

Similarly, you are free to use the icons and images in the samples. The images are designed to be a placeholder so that you know what size and shape you need to have for icons and start-up splash screens. Feel free to use the Photoshop files as a starting place to create your own images that actually look nice. I've intentionally made them look kind of ugly to discourage you from actually using them in a real app.

Language Choices

To all of you Visual Basic lovers out there: I sympathize with you. I developed using VB for almost 15 years and loved it, starting with VB3, but I made the jump to C# a few years ago because of my clients. All of the samples in this book are in C# because it seems to be the prevalent language nowadays.

Chapter 1   I Love MVC 4!

"This is your last chance. After this, there is no turning back. You take the blue pill—the story ends, you wake up in your bed and believe whatever you want to believe. You take the red pill—you stay in Wonderland and I show you how deep the rabbit hole goes."
   Morpheus in *The Matrix*

I've been writing websites for many years. Back in 1997, I wrote my first e-commerce website for a local printing company using Cold Fusion 1.0 and I thought that product was awesome at the time. I moved on to a company that developed a lot of websites during the infamous dot-com bubble which went bankrupt a few years later. During that time, we did a lot of Classic ASP development and I found a lot to like in that model. We alternated back and forth between ASP and Cold Fusion depending on what we needed. During those early years of websites and e-commerce 1.0, we learned a lot about how to streamline websites. With people hitting sites using a 9600 baud modem, it had to be as small and efficient as possible, and 100 KB was our upper limit for page size.

In 2002, Microsoft released ASP.NET, and developers had to learn a totally new system that was very different than the ASP we had just mastered. This new model looked a lot like the Windows Forms programming model and once we got over the learning curve, life was good for a while. We learned about the evils of the ViewState and Session management and all the things that could trip you up and bloat your page. But as connections got faster, it really didn't bother us too much that our pages started to put on a little extra weight.

One of the things that has always bothered me about ASP.NET Web Forms is the HTML it generates—have you ever taken a good look at that? Trying to trace through that code was a nightmare. When creating JavaScript, the field names and IDs were always an issue. You always had to ask yourself, "Do I have to put a 'ctl100_' in front of this field?" But we put up with it because that's how ASP.NET worked and it was better than the alternative.

When the first versions of MVC came along, I wasn't too excited about them. It wasn't until I looked at MVC 3 and the new Razor syntax that I began to get interested. As I researched it more, I learned more about the new programming model that MVC projects bring to ASP.NET. There was a style and simplicity that reminded me of the good old days of Classic ASP, but with all of the new functionality and richness of a modern application.

Along with MVC 3 came the Entity Framework and Code First, and those particular ideas really resonated with me. My philosophy of programming tends to be what I refer to as "DDD"—Database-Driven Development. As I approach a project, I tend to think of things in terms of databases, models, and entities. I usually have a good idea in my head of how I can store the data for the application about the same time I start having a semi-rough screen design. MVC allowed me to follow my usual development path and opened up my development to many other possibilities. I fell in love.

I realize that MVC is not the ultimate development tool, and not everyone is going to love it. But as someone who has worked in web development in Microsoft-centered shops for many years, I have to say this is the best we've had it in a long time.

Chapter 2   Why a Book about Mobile-Friendly Websites?

"Toto, I've got a feeling we're not in Kansas anymore."
  Dorothy in *The Wizard of Oz*

A few years ago, mobile websites were just an afterthought unless you had a company that was developing an application designed specifically for a phone. It's hard to believe that the first iPhone was just released in 2007 (it seems longer than that)! Before then, our phones were used as, well, phones. Now they've become much more. Think of all the things that our cell phones have replaced: wristwatch, stopwatch, calendar, datebook, flashlight, email, map, gaming device, dictionary, encyclopedia, etc.

Google estimates that by 2013, more people will use mobile phones than PCs to get online.[1]   Wow! That's not far away. They also estimate that by 2015, there will be one mobile device for *every person on Earth*!

If you haven't started making your website mobile-friendly, you're **already** behind the curve. You need to start now. I recently had a friend tell me about how his company just had its website redesigned by a marketing firm. I asked him if it was mobile-friendly and he just looked at me with a blank stare. I whipped out my iPhone and typed in the site. It was a nice-looking site if you were sitting at a PC. Unfortunately, on my iPhone the font looked like it was about 0.5-point font, and much of the graphics were done in Flash so there were big blocks of nothing on the screen. The company just wasted a lot of money on that fancy new site and it will have to rebuild it again soon, probably shortly after its CEO gets an iPhone!

So what can you do to make sure that your website doesn't suffer the same fate? I'm going to show you how you can make your website more mobile-friendly if you are using MVC. If you are using other technologies, this may not be the book for you. You will probably learn a few things, but most of what I have to say is for MVC programmers. If that is your current paradigm, this book should help you tremendously. Most of the content is centered on MVC 4, but I'll also show you how you can use these techniques in MVC 3 in case you're stuck in that environment.

This isn't a book about learning MVC—I'm assuming you already know a fair bit about MVC and have done a little bit of programming with it. You don't have to be an expert in MVC, but this book isn't really going to explain how

MVC works. The focus will be on honing your MVC techniques so that your sites look good on mobile devices.

Chapter 3   Designing Mobile-Friendly Websites

"Mama always said life was like a box of chocolates. You never know what you're gonna get."
   Forrest Gump in *Forrest Gump*

Designing mobile websites is a big topic these days. Every conference you go to has several sessions on this topic, and there is an abundance of books on the topic. With all that noise, it's hard to know who to listen to.

Some folks are saying that you need to use a dedicated site for mobile and a separate site for desktop. This is sometimes referred to as the "mdot" strategy, because many sites put an "m." on the front of their mobile URL. However, this strategy causes a problem because you end up with two (or three!) different sites that you must maintain, each with duplicate content and web configurations.

Other sites rely on what is commonly known as Responsive Web Design. The theory is that if you design your site right with style sheets that adapt, you will be able to have one site with one URL, and it will adapt to many screen sizes, scaling the size up or down, shifting columns around, and making it look nice on all sorts of different sizes. One place this strategy fails miserably is page bloat. Even though you have a small screen with less visible content, you typically don't have **less content**. Less visible content does NOT equal fewer bytes downloaded. Phones have data caps and lower download speeds, so using that strategy is not the most optimal design for mobile devices.

If you design a website using the responsive design strategy, you need to decide if you are going to start with a mobile design as your bias and then do progressive enhancement as the screen gets larger, or if you want to start with the desktop design, and then do graceful degradation. Both approaches suffer from some serious issues.

What if you could create a site that took good parts from both of these strategies? Rather than relying on the Responsive Web Design strategy, I prefer to use a pattern that I refer to as "Adaptive View Design." By using the Adaptive View Design patterns in this book, you can have parts of the best of both of these strategies in your project.

Desktop Layout versus Mobile Layout

Before we get into the actual code, there are several design concepts that need to be understood when you are designing a mobile layout. There are some obvious differences when you compare a desktop screen to a small phone screen, and there are some that are not as obvious when you are designing for a medium-sized screen like a tablet.

Multicolumn versus Single-Column Design

When you design a typical desktop website, you tend to work with a multicolumn layout with the three-column layout being the most common approach. Such a layout utilizes banner images, menu bars, ads to grab your attention, etc., like this:

Banner Image		
Menu Bar		
Detailed Sub-Menu	Actual Content	Ads Ads Ads Ads ...

Desktop Layout

When laying out a mobile website, a better approach is to design for a single-column layout. Using just one column makes it easy to scale between differently sized devices and makes it simple to switch between portrait and landscape mode. Consider the layout of most phone applications:

Phone Layout

On the other hand, tablets tend to have a little bit of both approaches. A tablet tends to favor the one column approach common to phones, but then it will switch to a two-column layout when rotated to landscape mode, and only occasionally will it use a three-column layout.

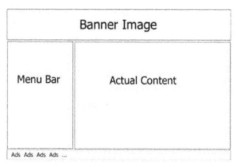

Tablet Layout

Each of the designs has a different approach, and it would be a mistake to assume that we could create one page that will work well in all three of these form factors. It's not just the layout that changes, either; there are other considerations.

Tapping versus Hovering and Clicking

Another issue to consider is that on a desktop people are used to clicking on little text links that take them to the next page, and a mouse is a very precise tool for doing that. On a mobile device, people are tapping with their fingers and thumbs, and a small text link doesn't really work when you are trying to do that. Your mobile-friendly design needs to incorporate larger buttons and icons wherever possible, and use links that let you tap anywhere on the whole line to activate a choice, not just on the actual word that contains the link.

In addition, on many desktop applications and websites, developers tend to use information that is hidden until the pointer hovers over an object. That concept simply doesn't exist on a touch-based input device like a phone or tablet.

Large Screens and Collapsible Containers

In addition to scaling back the number of columns in your design, you need to think about the content containers themselves. On a desktop there is plenty of real estate, so it makes sense to expand and show as much data as you can inside many visually distinct containers. On the small screen of a mobile device, you want to show the least amount of data that makes sense, and then have the user decide what to show next, and on a tablet it's somewhere between. One of the options that is most sensible for this paradigm is the collapsible container. The following three screenshots are the exact same URL with the exact same contents, but each of them is organized and optimized for the platform it is targeting.

Desktop View

In this example, the desktop shows all of the content, and it's organized into nice containers with appropriate styling.

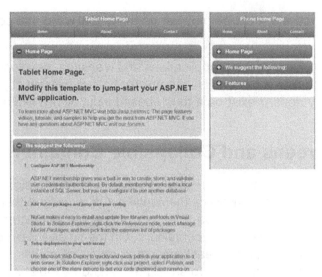

Tablet and Phone Views

The tablet view shows the same content, but it is placed inside containers that have a minus sign in the header that allow you to collapse them if you want. The phone view uses those same containers, but starts with everything collapsed so you can easily scan the document for what interests you.

> In *Chapter 8*, we'll look at a pattern that we can use where you can have three distinct layouts, but reuse the same content in each of the layouts so that you don't end up with duplicate content. We'll also look at the collapsible containers in more detail in *Chapters 8* and *9*.

Desktop != Tablet != Phone

Hopefully this chapter has made you think just a little bit about the different design paradigms that need to be addressed when building mobile websites. Good desktop design is not the same as good tablet design, and that's not the same thing as good phone design. The key here is to try to optimize the design to match the device requesting the content, and at the same time not have to maintain duplicate content in multiple sites and files.

When it comes to designing websites, Forrest Gump was right—we don't really know what we're going to get. We might think we know how we should design our site, but before we know it, a new device is going to come along and surprise us. As someone once said, "If you make something idiot proof, they'll just make a better idiot."

Chapter 4   Building an MVC Mobile Website

Frodo: "Go back, Sam. I'm going to Mordor alone."
Sam: "Of course you are. And I'm coming with you."
  From *The Lord of the Rings: The Fellowship of the Ring*

MVC 3 has the ability to create mobile-friendly code, but it isn't a built-in feature. You have to write your own custom code and put it in the project, and it isn't straightforward.

> We'll discuss how to create a mobile-friendly website using MVC 3 in Chapter 11, but our main focus here is MVC 4.

MVC 4 comes with the ability to turn on mobile support with just a few little lines of code in your application startup—it's really simple to do. Let's take a journey into the world of MVC 4 and mobile.

The Mobile Application Template

When you install MVC 4[2] and create your first project, you will immediately gravitate toward the **Mobile Application** template. It seems like the first thing you would go to, and you *might* be right. Let's take a look at what it generates and see how that works out.

When you select this option, the template will generate a mobile website for you, and it will include the jQuery and jQuery.Mobile environments. jQuery.Mobile is one of the key components to easily making your website mobile-friendly. jQuery.Mobile is a framework built on top of jQuery that is designed to help you make mobile user interfaces. It doesn't replace jQuery —it builds on it and enhances it. Spend a little time browsing the jQuery.Mobile site[3], and you will find that they have spent a lot of time making it very easy to create mobile-friendly websites that play nicely on a variety of devices. The Microsoft team was wise to adopt this open-source project.

> *The examples in this book are designed with jQuery.Mobile version 1.1, which was released in April, 2012. If you have a newer version (or even a slightly older like version 1.0.1), the concepts in this book should still apply, as most of the changes are enhancements and not breaking changes.*

If you take this default project template and run it, you'll see something like this:

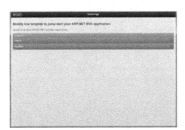

Website Created with the Mobile Template

That's not bad for a first start. However, there is one small problem with this approach: there is no desktop version! This one serves up the mobile version to each and every device that comes to this website. It's not mobile-friendly; it's mobile-only.

If you think back to the previous chapter, and consider what you are trying to accomplish when building a mobile-friendly website, you will soon come to realize that you need to pay attention to three different form factors: small, medium, and large.

Form Factors to Consider for Mobile-Friendly Websites

And let's not forget what's coming your way in 2013! Like it or not, you may have to think about this new format sooner than you think...

Project Glass, Anyone?

Trying to create one design that is going to work for all of these is usually an exercise in futility and will produce something that doesn't work well on two out of three. We need some way to optimize our designs for each of the different platforms. Fortunately, that's not too hard to do with the MVC platform.

The Internet Application Template

Let's start again, and this time we'll pick the **Internet Application** template. What we will get now is a website that is primarily optimized for the desktop platform. We'll work with that and then enhance it to make it more mobile-friendly.

When you build and run this website, it will look almost exactly the same on your mobile device as it does on your desktop, as shown in the following pictures. Notice that in the mobile device view, the content has used a bit of responsive web design and re-flowed itself a bit to make it look a *little* bit better in that format.

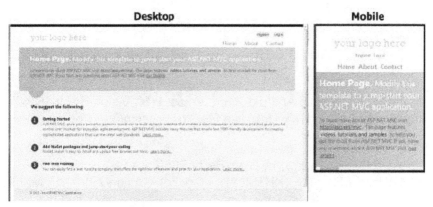

Website Created with the Internet Application Template

For some websites, your mobile phone only shows a version of the site shrunk down to fit the screen of your mobile device (like my friend's website that I mentioned in the first chapter). So why doesn't our site based on the **Internet Application** template shrink down to a tiny version of itself? This template has avoided that problem by including one little line of magic code in its main layout page (look at **\Views\Shared_Layout.cshtml**):

```
<meta name="viewport" content="width=device-width" />
```

That's it! The WebKit-based browsers used in the majority of mobile phones (like Android and iPhones) will respect that tag and will automatically try to resize and reflow the content to fit on the width of the current device. That's one little tidbit you can apply to just about any website you are working on right now. *(Go ahead. Go try it now on your current project. This book can wait. I know you want to.)*

OK—are you back? Did it work? There are several other `<meta>` tags that we'll discuss in Chapter 7 that can make your website more mobile-friendly—this is the first of many.

Our goal was to return different content to different types of devices. To do that, we will have to know what type of device is making the request, and for that we will look at the user agent. You probably already know that every time a browser sends a request to our server, it also sends a `User-Agent` string along with that request which identifies to the server what application is requesting the information. There are many different strings you might see. Here are a few examples:

- Mozilla/5.0 (iPhone; U; CPU iPhone OS 4_3_3 like Mac OS X; en-us) AppleWebKit/533.17.9 (KHTML, like Gecko) Version/5.0.2 Mobile/8J2 Safari/6533.18.5

- Mozilla/5.0 (iPad; U; CPU OS 4_3_3 like Mac OS X; en-us) AppleWebKit/533.17.9 (KHTML, like Gecko) Version/5.0.2 Mobile/8J2 Safari/6533.18.5

- Mozilla/5.0 (Linux; U; Android 2.3.5; en-us; HTC Vision Build/GRI40) AppleWebKit/533.1 (KHTML, like Gecko) Version/4.0 Mobile Safari/533.1

- Mozilla/5.0 (BlackBerry; U; BlackBerry 9850; en-US) AppleWebKit/534.11+ (KHTML, like Gecko) Version/7.0.0.115 Mobile Safari/534.11+

- BlackBerry9700/5.0.0.862 Profile/MIDP-2.1 Configuration/CLDC-1.1 VendorID/167

- Mozilla/5.0 (compatible; MSIE 9.0; Windows NT 7.1; Trident/5.0)

- Mozilla/5.0 (compatible; MSIE 9.0; Windows NT 6.1; WOW64; Trident/5.0; SLCC2; Media Center PC 6.0; InfoPath.3; MS-RTC LM 8; Zune 4.7)

We can use this information to make our website respond to different devices in a different way. In the next section, I'll walk through all of the code needed to make this work.

Simulating a Mobile Device for Testing

Before we start on that, let's take a detour and see how you can easily simulate a mobile device on your desktop. The easiest way that I have found is to use the Apple Safari browser. Once you've installed it, go to the **Preferences** settings and select the **Advanced** tab.

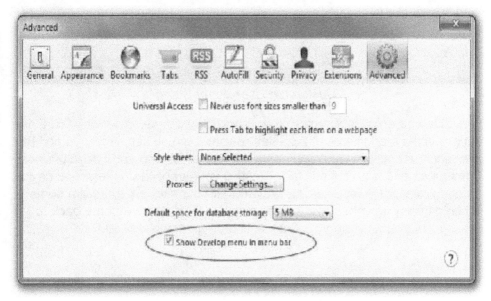

Advanced Tab under Preferences in Safari

Make sure that the **Show Develop menu** check box is selected and you're almost ready. Remember discussing different user agent strings previously? Here is where you put them to use. Safari will let you easily change the user agent that it supplies to a website if you have the **Develop menu** setting turned on. Just go to the newly enabled **Develop** menu item and pick one.

User Agents Available in Safari

If you are interested in seeing the details for one of the user agent strings, just select it and let it refresh your page, then come back to this menu and select the **Other…** option. Your currently selected user agent will be displayed and you can edit it.

Customize User Agent String

If you want to emulate an Android or BlackBerry device, you won't find those options in the menu items of Apple's browser, but you can simply go find the user agent string you want and paste it into this box and you'll be in business. Remember, this is no substitute for testing your website on the actual device. It does provide a quick and dirty way to test your site, but there are some subtle differences in behavior on the mobile device that will come back to haunt you if you don't do your final testing on an actual device.

Visual Studio 2012 features a convenient toolbar option for choosing a browser to run your application.

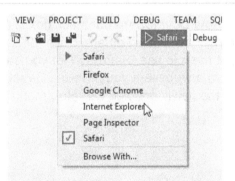

Choosing a Browser in Visual Studio 2012

Recognizing Mobile Devices

Let's get back to our main topic and enable our code to recognize different types of mobile devices. Open the **Global.asax.cs** file and go to the `Application_Start` method, and then insert the `DisplayModeProvider` code below that is shown after the `BundleConfig.RegisterRoutes` line:

```
using System.Web.WebPages;

protected void Application_Start()
{
  AreaRegistration.RegisterAllAreas();
  FilterConfig.RegisterGlobalFilters(GlobalFilters.Filters);
  RouteConfig.RegisterRoutes(RouteTable.Routes);
  BundleConfig.RegisterBundles(BundleTable.Bundles);

  DisplayModeProvider.Instance.Modes.Insert(0,
    new DefaultDisplayMode("Phone")
  {
    ContextCondition = (context => (
      (context.GetOverriddenUserAgent() != null) &&
      (
        (context.GetOverriddenUserAgent().IndexOf("iPhone",
          StringComparison.OrdinalIgnoreCase) >= 0) ||
        (context.GetOverriddenUserAgent().IndexOf("iPod",
          StringComparison.OrdinalIgnoreCase) >= 0) ||
        (context.GetOverriddenUserAgent().IndexOf("Droid",
          StringComparison.OrdinalIgnoreCase) >= 0) ||
        (context.GetOverriddenUserAgent().IndexOf("Blackberry",
          StringComparison.OrdinalIgnoreCase) >= 0) ||
        (context.GetOverriddenUserAgent()
          .StartsWith("Blackberry",
            StringComparison.OrdinalIgnoreCase))
      )
    ))
  });

  DisplayModeProvider.Instance.Modes.Insert(0,
    new DefaultDisplayMode("Tablet")
  {
    ContextCondition = (context => (
      (context.GetOverriddenUserAgent() != null) &&
      (
        (context.GetOverriddenUserAgent().IndexOf("iPad",
          StringComparison.OrdinalIgnoreCase) >= 0) ||
        (context.GetOverriddenUserAgent().IndexOf("Playbook",
          StringComparison.OrdinalIgnoreCase) >= 0) ||
        (context.GetOverriddenUserAgent()
          .IndexOf("Transformer",
            StringComparison.OrdinalIgnoreCase) >= 0) ||
        (context.GetOverriddenUserAgent().IndexOf("Xoom",
          StringComparison.OrdinalIgnoreCase) >= 0)
      )
    ))
  });

}
```

I've inserted the two blocks of code that start with **DisplayModeProvider** (plus a **using System.Web.WebPages;** statement at the top of the file). These lines set up a new entry in the available **DisplayModes** table for this application. Each time a request is received by the application, it is evaluated to determine how that request should be formatted when it is processed. In this case, if the conditions are matched for one of these custom modes, then the name of that mode is injected into the name of the file. The conditions specified in the previous code sample look at the user agent string and check to see if there is a match.

For instance, if the client is an iPhone, it would send in a user agent string similar to this:

```
Mozilla/5.0 (iPhone; U; CPU iPhone OS 4_3_3 like Mac OS X; en-us)
AppleWebKit/533.17.9 (KHTML, like Gecko) Version/5.0.2 Mobile/8J2
Safari/6533.18.5
```

Our application would then match that up and determine that it should use the `Phone` display mode. The MVC engine would then look at the view it was creating and slightly modify the file it was looking for:

What the client requested: */YourApp/SomeController/*

The view a PC would get is based on: */Views/SomeController/Index.cshtml*

The view an iPhone would get is based on: */Views/SomeController/Index.Phone.cshtml*

When the controller builds up the HTML to return to the phone, it will base the request on the **Index.Phone.cshtml** file. With that information, we can easily create unique views that are designed specifically for the type of device that is browsing our site. Make two copies of the **Home/Index.cshtml** file and rename them to **Index.Phone.cshtml** and **Index.Tablet.cshtml**.

Some purists will be certain to point out that there are libraries out there like WURFL or 51Degrees that do a much better job of determining exactly which device is requesting the page and what capabilities it has, rather than the user-agent sniffing code listed previously, and they have a good point. However, this code hits about 99% of what is needed with extremely small overhead and very limited maintenance upkeep. If you're worried about that other 1%, go ahead and investigate other options. Otherwise, this code will do the job fairly well with a lot less muss and fuss.

Including jQuery.Mobile

The first step in creating a truly different look and feel for each mobile device is to include the **jQuery.Mobile** package in our project. You can do this by opening up the **Package Manager Console** under **Tools** > **Library Package Manager** > **Package Manager Console**, and typing the following line: *Install-Package jQuery.Mobile*.

```
PM> Install-Package jQuery.Mobile

Attempting to resolve dependency 'jquery (≥ 1.6.4)'.

Successfully installed 'jQuery 1.6.4'.

Successfully installed 'jquery.mobile 1.1.0'.

Successfully removed 'jQuery 1.6.2' from Chapter4.

Successfully added 'jQuery 1.6.4' to Chapter4.

Successfully added 'jquery.mobile 1.1.0' to Chapter4.

Successfully uninstalled 'jQuery 1.6.2'.
```

> *If you're not a command line junkie like me, you can use the GUI under Tools > Library Package Manager > Manage NuGet Packages for Solution and search for jQuery.Mobile. They both do exactly the same thing.*

That's step one, but it doesn't do much for you yet. If you run your project now, it will look exactly the same, with one minor difference: you should see a sliding transition animation when you switch between pages. Ignore that for now and we will come back to fix that in a few minutes.

Creating a Mobile Layout Page

The next step is to set up a unique **Layout** page for those mobile devices. In your **\Views\Shared** folder, you should find a **_Layout.cshtml** file, which is what all of your pages are based off of at this point. (*This is analogous to the master page for all you ASP.NET Web Forms programmers out there.*) Copy that file to a new **\Views\Shared_Layout.Phone.cshtml** file and that's where we will start our customization.

When you open that up, you will see a few lines that look like this:

```
@Styles.Render("~/Content/themes/base/css", "~/Content/css")
@Scripts.Render("~/bundles/modernizr")
```

MVC 4 Bundles

The bundling feature is one of the new features of MVC 4 that you will really appreciate. If you have ever tried to optimize your website performance in previous versions of MVC 3 and ASP.NET, one of the things that you had to focus on was to minimize the number of web requests and to reduce the size of the data that was requested. In order to do this, there were several programs available that could minimize and concatenate any JavaScript or style sheets into one smaller file. For example, you might use the following scripts: **jquery-1.6.4.min.js**, **jquery-ui.js**, **jquery.validate.js**, and **jquery.validate.unobtrusive.js**. You could use the minimized versions of each of these (***.min.js**) and considerably reduce the amount of data that you would download to your device, but it would still make four HTTP requests for these four files. By concatenating these files together, you could reduce it to one HTTP request. If you are running a PC on a local network, such as a developer using his or her desktop or testing against a local server, you would never notice the time it took to load those four files. On a mobile device that is running on a 3G (or 1G) network, this could amount to a huge increase in load time for the page.

MVC 4 attempts to alleviate this problem by providing you with a simple built-in way of combining and minifying files through use of a **Bundle**. By using the `BundleUrl` option, you can simply point to a directory and tell the page that you want everything in that directory lumped together into one file, and MVC will do it for you automatically.

That's awesome—I love new features that do something for me that I used to have to do manually! However...

Creating a Custom Bundle

Sometimes those helpful things for your production site make it more difficult for you to develop. In our project, we have just included the jQuery.Mobile package. I mentioned that once we included jQuery.Mobile in our project, the desktop views would have sliding transitions, and we may not want that. We want those scripts to apply to our mobile pages, but not to change our desktop pages. So the question is how do we separate those files out into desktop and mobile versions and load only the files that we want?

Let's see how we can create some custom bundles in our application by adding a bit of custom code in the new MVC 4 **BundleConfig.cs** file located in the **App_Start** folder. We'll modify the `RegisterBundles` function to handle that. We'll create a couple of custom bundles for our mobile version and specify only the files we are interested in.

Here is the code:

```
public static void RegisterBundles(BundleCollection bundles)
{
  [... existing bundle code goes here... ]

  bundles.Add(new ScriptBundle("~/bundles/MobileJS").Include(
    "~/Scripts/jquery.mobile-1.*",
    "~/Scripts/jquery-1.*"));

  bundles.Add(new StyleBundle("~/Content/MobileCSS").Include(
    "~/Content/jquery.mobile.structure-1.1.0.min.css",
    "~/Content/jquery.mobile-1.1.0.css"));
#if DEBUG
  BundleTable.EnableOptimizations = false;
#else
  BundleTable.EnableOptimizations = true;
#endif
}
```

If you are writing and debugging your own JavaScript and including those files in your bundles, you may want to control when that code gets minified so that it's easier to debug. If the `compilation` tag in your **Web.config** is set to `debug=true`, no minification will take place. Alternatively, you can explicitly set the `BundleTable.EnableOptimizations` tag in your code in `RegisterBundles`, and that will control it as well and will override the **Web.config** settings.

Web.config Setting

```
<system.web>
    <compilation debug="true" />
</system.web>
```

Now that we have our bundles created, let's put them into our layout files. Open your **_Layout.Phone.cshtml** file and replace the `bundles/jquery` tag with the new `MobileJS` tag and replace the `css` bundle with the new `MobileCSS` tag, like this:

Before

```
<!DOCTYPE html>

<html lang="en">

    <head>
```

```
        <meta charset="utf-8" />

        ...

        ...

    @Styles.Render("~/Content/css")

    @Scripts.Render("~/bundles/modernizr")

    </head>

    <body>

        ...

        ...

    @Scripts.Render("~/bundles/jquery")

    @RenderSection("scripts", required: false)

    </body>

</html>
```

After

```
<!DOCTYPE html>

<html lang="en">

    <head>

        <meta charset="utf-8" />

            ...

        ...

    @Styles.Render("~/Content/MobileCSS")

    @Scripts.Render("~/bundles/modernizr")

    @Scripts.Render("~/bundles/MobileJS")

    </head>

    <body>

        ...

        ...

    @RenderSection("scripts", required: false)

    </body>
```

```
</html>
```

Save these changes, and then copy the **_Layout.Phone.cshtml** file and rename the copy **_Layout.Tablet.cshtml**. We'll update it later with more features to differentiate the two types of layouts, but this will work for now. Let's run our application and see what we have so far.

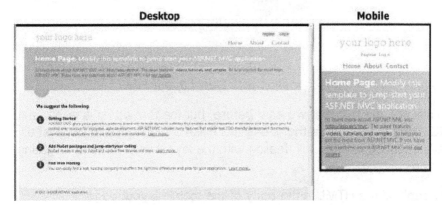

Desktop and Mobile Application Views

Using Our New Layout Files

Why hasn't our site changed? It hasn't changed because although we have created new layout files, we aren't using them yet in any of our pages. To use a custom layout for any of your views, you need to add one line of code to the top of your view. In this case, edit the **Index.Phone.cshtml** file and add this line at the top:

```
@{ Layout = "../Shared/_Layout.Phone.cshtml"; }
```

Then edit the **Index.Tablet.cshtml** file and add this line at the top:

```
@{ Layout = "../Shared/_Layout.Tablet.cshtml"; }
```

Now try running it again while using a phone or tablet user agent, and you should see something that looks like this:

Application with New Layout Files

You still see the text that we saw before, but the formatting is gone, and we STILL don't have a page that looks much like a mobile-friendly website. That's because we are still dealing with the layout of a website targeting desktops.

Let's replace the HTML in the body of the mobile layout page (**_Layout.Phone.cshtml**) with some code that is much simpler and is designed for mobile devices and jQuery.Mobile:

```
<body>
  <div data-role="page" data-theme="b">
    <div data-role="header" data-theme="b">
      <h1>@ViewBag.Title</h1>
    </div>
    <div data-role="content" data-theme="d">
      <nav>
        <ul id="menu">
          <li>@Html.ActionLink("Home", "Index", "Home")</li>
          <li>@Html.ActionLink("About", "About", "Home")</li>
          <li>@Html.ActionLink("Contact", "Contact", "Home")</li>
        </ul>
      </nav>
@RenderSection("featured", false)
@RenderBody()
    </div>
  </div>
</body>
```

This page has most of the same content sections as the **_Layout.cshtml** page but is formatted quite differently. Pay special attention to the `data` tags on the `page`, `header`, and `content divs`. Those are special tags to jQuery.Mobile. They give jQuery.Mobile more information about how to deal with these sections. There will be many `data` tags that you can use to customize your page, and we'll see some of them shortly.

With this new layout in place, let's try once more and see if our site is starting to take shape:

Application with Improved Appearance for Mobile Devices

That's much better. It's still not quite 100% there yet, but it's starting to get there. We can see from this quick example that we are getting a page that is starting to look different from our desktop version. In the next section, we'll continue customizing this page to enhance the look even further.

To sum this up, here is a short checklist of what we have done so far to make all this work:

1. Created an MVC 4 project based on the **Internet Template**.

2. Added the `DisplayModeProvider` code to the **Global.asax** to detect a phone or a tablet user agent.

3. Included **jQuery.Mobile** in the project.

4. Created a custom bundle so the mobile scripts wouldn't affect the desktop pages.

5. Created a custom **Layout** page in the **Shared** folder for a phone and a tablet.

6. Created a phone and tablet version of each page and changed them to use the new layouts.

7. Tested the site with Safari and a custom user agent.

That's quite a list, isn't it? I bet you're thinking that this isn't as easy as I promised it was going to be. In this chapter, you've been learning to walk so that later you can run. This process works much better if you understand the steps that need to take place so you don't trip and fall when you start to run.

One of the nice new features in Visual Studio introduced with MVC 4 is the addition of recipes, which can help you automate many of these steps. By using a recipe like Lyle's MVC 4 FoodTruck Recipe (available at http://nuget.org/packages/LCI.FoodTruck.MVC4/), you can automate most of these steps and make this entire process painless. I've done demos with this recipe where I've created a SQL Server database, added a table and data (by running a SQL script), then created a full website with desktop and mobile views in about 10 minutes. However, before you can do that, you need to understand all the steps involved first.

Chapter 5   Making It Mobile-Friendly

"Make everything as simple as possible, but not simpler."
Albert Einstein

With the changes we made in the previous chapter, we now have a site that is starting to look a little bit more like a mobile-friendly website, but there are still several issues that remain. If we use our demo site and scroll the page up and down, you'll see that the header scrolls off the page and disappears, and the list doesn't really have any graphical flair like a mobile-styled list should have. There are many things we could address, but let's start by fixing those two things.

Fixing the Headers

Currently the header is attached to the top of the page. If you scroll the page, the header disappears. Adding a **data-position** tag to the header makes that header stick at the top of the page when you scroll up or down.

```
<div data-role="header" data-position="fixed" data-theme="b">
```

That's it! One of the great things about using jQuery.Mobile is that it has a lot of built-in features like this that you can use easily. With this tag in place, the header will stay at the top of the screen. If the user taps the screen, he or she can also make the header appear or disappear.

Styling Our List Objects

Next let's take a look at the menu and give that a little bit of visual pizazz. Adding the **data-role** and **data-inset** tags to the list header will make that list take on a new style. In addition, we can add a header to the list by using a **list-divider** item to give it a little more visual interest:

```
<nav>

  <ul data-role="listview" data-inset="true">

    <li data-role="list-divider">Menu Items</li>

    <li>@Html.ActionLink("Home", "Index", "Home")</li>

    <li>@Html.ActionLink("About", "About", "Home")</li>

    <li>@Html.ActionLink("Contact", "Contact", "Home")</li>

  </ul>

</nav>
```

By making these extremely small changes, we will have a much nicer looking page:

 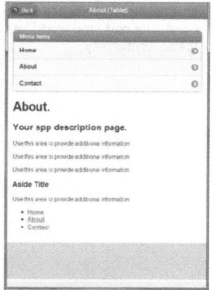

Improved Headers and Styling of List Items

Now we're making some progress toward making this site mobile-friendly.

While viewing the home page, click on the **About** page link and see what happens. One thing you will notice is that you can click anywhere on that line and the action will happen. You don't have to be restricted to just clicking on the word **About**.

If you've been following along (and not forging ahead on your own), when you click on the **About** link, you should see something like the right half of the previous image. Notice anything missing? You should notice that there is no back button in the header bar. Most mobile applications keep track of their context and provide you with a way to go back easily. You might be tempted to reply that the user can always just use the **Back** button in the browser, and that would work in many cases. But what if this goes into a full-screen web app mode? As you'll see in <u>Chapter 7</u>, we can set up our applications to take over the screen and emulate a native app, and in that case, there is no **Back** button, so we do need to deal with this.

Another thing that's very noticeable is that we're also showing the menu on the **Home** page and the **About** page, which is redundant. On a desktop, users expect to have that menu bar at the top of the screen. But you have to remember that this is a mobile device with a tiny screen—we want to maximize our real estate and only show information that is absolutely necessary on each page. Our goal here is to create a mobile-friendly site and also a desktop-friendly site at the same time, so we need to customize that as well. Our next step would be to remove that menu and add in the **Back** button functionality.

Detour: Why do we need three copies of everything?

Before we head down the path of adding in a **Back** button, let's take a quick side trip. Take a look at the **Views** folder and see if you notice anything that seems a bit unusual:

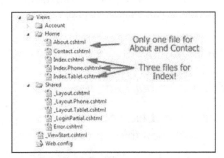

Views Folder Contents

When we created a mobile-friendly view of the **Index** page, we copied that file to **Index.Phone.cshtml** and **Index.Tablet.cshtml**, and put in special layout commands in each of those. We haven't done that yet with the **About** view, so how did that get a mobile view? And why do we even need these two extra files if the **About** page worked without them?

The answer is that by simply putting the layout files out there, any page that does not have a *.Phone or *.Tablet counterpart will load the default page, and if it matches up with our `DisplayMode` definitions it will use the **_Layout.Phone** or **_Layout.Tablet** layout file. That may or may not be what we want. If our goal is to create a unique experience across all three platforms, we'll want to supply a unique version of each file. That does lead to some maintenance issues if you have your content replicated three times, but we'll touch on how to address that in Chapter 8.

Adding Home and Back Buttons

For now, our number one goal is to put a **Back** button in our toolbar, so let's get back to that. Typically, there are two basic buttons you will expect to find in the upper left corner: a **Back** button or a **Home** button. Many times a **Back** button is all you need, but there are times when you don't want to go back to the previous screen so you want a fixed-behavior **Home** button. For example, if you present a list of editable items to a user, and then he or she edits an item and clicks **Save**, you don't want the user to click the **Back** button and be taken back to the edit screen they just left. The old data would still be present in the list, so we'll have to handle that scenario. *(Whew! We're getting a lot of things on our to-do list!)*

Let's start by editing our **Layout** file and adding code for an optional **Back** or **Home** button in the header. Open this file in the editor and insert the following code in the `div` with the `data-role=header`:

```
<div data-role="header" data-position="fixed" data-theme="b">
  <h1>@ViewBag.Title</h1>
@{
  bool ShowBackButton = false;
  bool ShowHomeButton = false;
  if (ViewBag.ShowBackButton != null &&
      ViewBag.ShowBackButton == true)
  {
    ShowBackButton = true;
  }
  if (ViewBag.ShowHomeButton != null &&
      ViewBag.ShowHomeButton == true)
  {
    ShowHomeButton = true;
  }
  if (ShowBackButton)
  {
    <a data-rel="back" data-role="button"
       data-transition="slide" data-direction="reverse"
       data-icon="back">Back</a>
  }
  if (ShowHomeButton)
  {
    <a href="@Url.Action("Index", "Home")" data-role="button"
       data-transition="slide" data-direction="reverse"
       data-icon="home">Home</a>
  }
}
</div>
```

The `data-rel="back"` tag is another special tag for jQuery.Mobile and prompts it to keep track of the current stack of pages. When you click on this button it will go back to the previous page (this is very similar to `onclick="history.back()"` in JavaScript that you are probably familiar with). The `transition`, `direction`, and `icon` tags decorate the button a bit more and give it some default behaviors.

There is also an alternative way of doing this. You can actually add a "`data-add-back-btn`" tag on the page `div` like this:

```
<div data-role="page" data-theme="b" data-add-back-btn="true">
  <div data-role="header" data-position="fixed" data-theme="b">
  <h1>@ViewBag.Title</h1>
</div>
```

Both of these work, but they do have one small gotcha: they use the stack within jQuery.Mobile, which changes depending on how the user arrives at the page. If the user bookmarks your secondary page then comes back to it later—guess what? The **Back** button in the second version will be gone if they navigate directly to the page, and if you use the first technique, the **Back** button will be there but it may not do anything. If that's a concern, you may want to use the **Home** button to link directly back to the home page.

Next we'll create a unique version of **About.cshtml** for our phone and tablet. Copy that file and paste it twice into the **Home** directory, and then rename those files to **About.Phone.cshtml** and **About.Tablet.cshtml**. Open them in the editor and insert the `Layout` assignment and the `ViewBag` setting (for either the `ShowBackButton` or the `ShowHomeButton`) so that the start of the file looks like the following code sample:

```
@{
  Layout = "../Shared/_Layout.Phone.cshtml";
  ViewBag.ShowBackButton = true;
}
@{ ViewBag.Title = "About"; }
<hgroup class="title">
  <h1>@ViewBag.Title.</h1>
  <h2>@ViewBag.Message</h2>
</hgroup>
...the rest of the file...
```

Do the same with the tablet version by inserting the following lines at the top so that it looks like the following code sample:

```
@{
  Layout = "../Shared/_Layout.Tablet.cshtml";
  ViewBag.ShowBackButton = true;
}
```

```
@{ ViewBag.Title = "About"; }
<hgroup class="title">
  <h1>@ViewBag.Title.</h1>
  <h2>@ViewBag.Message</h2>
</hgroup>
...the rest of the file...
```

That's it. Now when you try running it, you have a website that's finally *starting* to look a bit like a mobile application.

Application with Home and Back Buttons

In this chapter, we've added fixed headers, nice-looking menus, back and home buttons, and a few other things that make our website look a little bit more like a mobile app. We can extend it even further with a few more enhancements, but this is a good start with only a few lines of code.

Chapter 6   Making It Look Good

Marty: "Wait a minute, Doc. Ah... Are you telling me that you built a time machine...out of a DeLorean?"

Doc: "The way I see it, if you're gonna build a time machine into a car, why not do it with some style?"

From *Back to the Future*

jQuery.Mobile Sections

jQuery.Mobile uses a fairly simple structure for defining its page elements. By using `data-role` tags on a `<div>`, they define these basic areas: `page`, `header`, `content`, `footer`, and `navbar`.

There are other areas that are defined and we'll talk about them in Chapter 9, but these are the basic ones that you will use often.

The Page Section

```
<div data-role="page" data-theme="b">
```

This is the main section of the document that jQuery.Mobile uses to wrap around all of the following sections. Typically it will include a `header`, `content`, and `footer` section, but only the `content` section is required. The `page` element itself is not actually required. However, if you do not supply one the framework will add one, so it is a best practice to go ahead and define it.

The Header Section

```
<div data-role="header" data-position="fixed" data-theme="b">
  <h1>@ViewBag.Title</h1>
</div>
```

This section contains the information that should be shown in the header of the page. The optional `data-position` element can make this element stick to the top when the user scrolls the page. You can see here that I've shown the typical MVC `Title` tag so it will automatically display the page title in the header. Space is limited, so the title will be cropped if it doesn't fit. We can insert any HTML we want here, but best practice is to use an `<h1>` for the title (You can also replace this with an image if you want something fancier). If you add one button in the `header div`, it will automatically move to the left side. If you add a second button, it will move to the right side automatically. You probably don't want more than two buttons as any others will move to the second line and make the header bigger (use a `navbar` instead).

The Content Section

```
<div data-role="content" data-theme="d">
  @RenderBody()
</div>
```

This is the section where you will put most of your content. In the code sample I've shown the typical MVC tag that will render your view content.

The Footer Section

```
<div data-role="footer" data-position="fixed" data-theme="b">
```

The **footer** is very similar to the **header**, except maybe a little more flexible. We can put more than two buttons here, and they will be added inline, one after the other (not left aligned and right aligned like the header). By default, the footer isn't formatted much, so you may have to add some other tags to make it look nice.

The Navbar Section

```
<div data-role="navbar">
```

This is a great place to put your navigation items. If you think about the normal desktop or Windows application design, we tended to use a lot of tab controls to group together related tab pages. This section provides you with a similar way of linking those pages together easily. If you put this into a partial view file, you can easily include it on any page that needs it. We'll discuss this in more detail in the next section.

Putting Your Menu into a Tab Bar

Let's convert the menu we started with into a fixed tab bar like you see at the bottom of most mobile applications, complete with icons. Currently, we have the following code on the home page of the mobile application for our menu items:

```
<ul data-role="listview" data-inset="true">
  <li data-role="list-divider">Menu Items</li>
  <li>@Html.ActionLink("Home", "Index", "Home")</li>
  <li>@Html.ActionLink("About", "About", "Home")</li>
  <li>@Html.ActionLink("Contact", "Contact", "Home")</li>
</ul>
```

Copy that code into a new file in our **Shared** folder and name it **_NavBar.cshtml**. Remove the fancy **<ul>** tag attributes and the **list-divider** row, and then wrap that in a **div** with the **navbar** tag we just looked at.

```
<div data-role="navbar" data-theme="b">
  <ul>
    <li>@Html.ActionLink("Home", "Index", "Home")</li>
    <li>@Html.ActionLink("About", "About", "Home")</li>
    <li>@Html.ActionLink("Contact", "Contact", "Home")</li>
  </ul>
</div>
```

Remove the original menu code from the **_Layout.Phone.cshtml** and **_Layout.Tablet.cshtml** and add in your new partial view to insert the new **navbar** we just created in the header.

```
<div data-role="header" data-position="fixed" data-theme="b">
  <h1>@ViewBag.Title</h1>
  @Html.Partial("_NavBar")
</div>
```

Since we already have the **data-position=fixed** on the header tag, this header and navigation bar will always remain at the top of the page.

If you want to add icons to your navigation, simply add a **data-icon** tag to each of the links. jQuery.Mobile contains several built-in icons that you can use: **arrow-l**, **arrow-r**, **arrow-u**, **arrow-d**, **delete**, **plus**, **minus**, **check**, **gear**, **refresh**, **forward**, **back**, **grid**, **star**, **alert**, **info**, **home**, or **search**. You can add a **data-iconpos** tag on the **navbar div** to determine where to show the icons. Valid values for the **iconpos** tag include **top**, **bottom**, **left**, or **right**.

To make this example a little easier to read when putting this extra tag into our links, we'll change them from `@Html.ActionLinks` to `hrefs` with `@URL.Action` tags, like this:

```
<div data-role="navbar" data-theme="b" data-iconpos="top">
  <ul>
    <li><a href="@Url.Action("Index", "Home")"
      data-icon="home">Home</a></li>
    <li><a href="@Url.Action("About", "Home")"
      data-icon="info">About Us</a></li>
    <li><a href="@Url.Action("Contact", "Home")"
      data-icon="check">Contact Us</a></li>
  </ul>
</div>
```

And that's it—we're all set to run the app and see how it works.

Menu Added in a Tab Bar

If you'd prefer to put your tab bar at the bottom of the page, you can put it in a `footer` section as shown in the following code sample:

```
<div data-role="footer" data-position="fixed" data-theme="b">
  @Html.Partial("_NavBar")
</div>
```

Either way works just fine—it's more of a style preference for your website.

Other Tab Bar Considerations

There are a few limitations for the tab bar that you need to know about. If you specify up to five buttons, you should be fine (although your text may be cut off on a phone, so keep the text short). If you have more than six buttons, the navbar will switch to a mode where it has multiple lines with two buttons on each line. It is usually a good idea to keep a tab bar to five buttons or less.

If you want to use your own custom icons that are not in the standard jQuery.Mobile set, that's actually fairly easy to do. We'll talk about how to do that in Chapter 9.

If you want to have one of the icons light up when you are on that page, you can use the tag `class="ui-btn-active"` on that link.

> *If you are using a shared partial view navbar, this gets a little more difficult but can be done by querying the* `Model.GetType()` *attribute. Using that, you can determine what type of model is being passed to the page and therefore what page you are on and which button should be highlighted.*

Alternate Syntax for the Navbar Links

In our previous example, we used the `@Url.Action` verb instead of `@HTML.ActionLink` because it makes it a little simpler to understand the example at first glance. It is possible to use either verb, but the `ActionLink` ends up being a little more complicated. Let's see an example of it in action:

```
<div data-role="navbar" data-theme="b" data-iconpos="top">
  <ul>
    <li>@Html.ActionLink("Home", "Index", "Home", null,
      new Dictionary<string, object> {{ "data-icon", "home" }})</li>
    <li>@Html.ActionLink("About Us", "About", "Home", null,
      new Dictionary<string, object> {{ "data-icon", "info" }})</li>
    <li>@Html.ActionLink("Contact Us", "Contact", "Home", null,
      new Dictionary<string, object> {{ "data-icon", "check" }})</li>
  </ul>
</div>
```

If you've used MVC before, you're probably wondering why we don't use the simpler notation shown in the following code sample:

```
<li>@Html.ActionLink("About", "Home", null,
  new { data-icon = "home" })</li>
```

This is the notation MVC programmers frequently use to pass an ID value into an action. However, if you try to do this with a name like `data-icon`, you get the error "Invalid anonymous type member declarator." If you translate that into English, that means, "You can't use a name with hyphens." Behind the scenes, our shortcut `"new {}"` code actually creates a dictionary for the `ActionLink` method. So in this case we can just go ahead and create a dictionary ourselves and then everything works just fine. Either method creates the same end product so it's really a matter of personal preference.

Yet Another Alternate Navbar Syntax

There is one other possibility worth considering in this discussion of how to format these links.

```
<div data-role="navbar" data-theme="b" data-iconpos="top">
  <ul>
    <li>@Html.ActionLink("Home", "Index", "Home", null,
      new { data_icon = "home" })</li>
    <li>@Html.ActionLink("About Us", "About", "Home", null,
      new { data_icon = "info" })</li>
    <li>@Html.ActionLink("Contact Us", "Contact", "Home", null,
      new { data_icon = "check" })</li>
  </ul>
</div>
```

In MVC 3 and MVC 4, there is a feature that will automatically convert underscore characters (_) to hyphen characters (-) when they are specified in HTML attribute properties, since underscores are not legal in HTML attributes. Therefore, in this example, it would change our **data_icon** to **data-icon** in the final HTML. As with the last example, either method creates the same end product so it's a matter of personal preference.

> *My personal opinion is that the trick with the underscore works but is a bit misleading. When using it, you are assuming that other programmers know this little tidbit of knowledge; otherwise they would be a bit confused looking at this code. In reality they all generate the exact same HTML, so it comes down to personal preference.*

Creating Custom Themes and Colors

One of the really nice features in jQuery.Mobile is the support for themes. You can theme almost any section of your page by adding in the tag `data-theme="x"`, where `x` is the style that you want to use, from A-E. The default themes are shown in the following figure.

Default jQuery.Mobile Themes

These themes use a cascading system. If you specify a theme for a container, the items within that container will use the color scheme specified unless another theme is chosen for them.

Even if you only use the default theme set, you have a nice-looking set of options and several choices you can make. But what if you want to use your own colors to match with your graphics or your company logo? Fortunately, jQuery.Mobile has teamed up with Adobe to create the jQuery.Mobile ThemeRoller site. If you want to see some good examples of what you can do, check out http://jqmgallery.com.

To get started with the ThemeRoller, navigate your browser to http://jquerymobile.com/themeroller/ and you will see the theme editor, but with a very bland gray palette. However, it's easy to fix that. Click the **Import** button in the toolbar, click on the **Import Default Theme** link in the resulting pop-up, and then click the **Import** button, and voila—now you have the standard jQuery.Mobile themes to work with.

Now you can start customizing your palette of colors to match your perfect website. Make sure you have the appropriate swatch selected in the panel on the left, and then use the color pickers to adjust and fine-tune them. If you don't make sure you have the correct swatch selected in the panel, you may end up changing the global colors and have to start all over again.

Here is my tribute to the good old "Hot Dog Stand" theme (those of you old enough to remember Windows 3.1 may understand that reference, and you youngsters can Google it!):

Re-creation of the "Hot Dog Stand" Theme

> *If you are reading this on a Kindle e Ink device, it won't be obvious, but this is a hideous red and yellow color.*

When you are happy with your color choices, you're ready to download it to your computer to use. Click the **Download Theme** link at the top and give it a name—in this case we'll use *HotDogStand*. The download will give you a zip file that contains the style sheets plus some extra files, but we're really just interested in two files: **HotDogStand.css** and **HotDogStand.min.css**. Extract those two files to your **Content** folder and then include them in your project.

If you were following along earlier, we created a custom bundle that would be minimized for our mobile pages in the **BundleConfig.cs** file. Go back into that code and comment out the existing **jquery.mobile-1.1.0.css** file and replace it with the file you just downloaded while keeping the **jquery.mobile.structure** file in the bundle:

```
public static void RegisterBundles(BundleCollection bundles)
{
    [... existing bundle code goes here... ]

    bundles.Add(new StyleBundle("~/Content/MobileCSS").Include(
      "~/Content/HotDogStand.css",
      "~/Content/jquery.mobile.structure-1.1.0.min.css",
      //"~/Content/jquery.mobile-1.1.0.css"
```

```
));
```

With these minor changes, you should be ready to go.

> *If you didn't do a custom bundle, then you'll have to edit the mobile layout files and put a reference in there to your new file.*
>
> *If you're still using the standard bundle that came as the project default, you'll have to remove the jquery.mobile-1.1.0.css file from the directory (or rename it to end in something other than .css.)*

As with any sharp tool, the ThemeRoller can be dangerous in the untrained hand, so make sure you consult with your graphic designer. Show your graphic designer how to use this tool and you can simply import the style sheet he or she produces directly.

Chapter 7   Using Mobile Device Meta Tags

"The difference between the right word and the almost right word is the difference between lightning and a lightning bug."
   Mark Twain

There are several easy options for enhancing your website to make it function more like a mobile application. Earlier we looked at the `viewport` tag briefly. We'll look at it in more detail in this chapter, along with other special tags shown in the following code sample:

```
<meta name="viewport" content="width=device-width" />
<meta name="apple-touch-fullscreen" content="no" />
<meta name="apple-mobile-web-app-capable" content="no" />
<link rel="apple-touch-icon"
  href="~/Content/images/apple-touch-icon.png" />
<link rel="apple-touch-startup-image"
  href="~/Content/images/iPhone_Startup.png" />
```

The Viewport Tag

We briefly looked at the `viewport` tag previously, and it looked like this:

```
<meta name="viewport" content="width=device-width" />
```

This tag is fairly simple. It tells the webpage to always try to use the width of the device that is requesting the page. For example, the iPhone has a resolution of either 320 × 480 pixels or 640 × 960 pixels (depending on which model you are using—see the chart later in this chapter for more detailed iOS screen resolutions). Therefore, a request from an iPhone will use a width of 320 or 640, and it will try not to exceed that width. If your content is structured properly, then it will reformat to fit that dimension. If you go to a normal website that doesn't have this tag and the site is formatted to be 900 pixels or 1024 pixels wide (like most desktop-targeted sites), it will look tiny on a phone. Unless it has this tag, it will continue to zoom out until the content fits on the screen.

If you use a header image wider than your device, then you may have a problem. If you specify a `style` tag on your image like **<img style="width: 100%;"… />** you should be okay. If you don't have that type of `style` tag, your page size will expand to the size of the image (even if you have a `viewport` tag), and the user may end up scrolling left and right.

There are a few other attributes on the `viewport` tag that you can use if needed:

```
<meta name="viewport" content="width=device-width, initial-scale=1.0, maximum-scale=1.0, user-scalable=no"/>
```

The `user-scalable` tag determines whether you will allow the user to pinch-zoom at all. The `initial-scale` sets the size of the page when it loads, and the `maximum-scale` defines how much the user will be able to zoom in. Both tags are set on a scale from 0 to 10.0. Typically you'll either set them to 1.0, or set the `maximum-scale` to a value like 3.0.

For more info, search the Apple Developer website[4] for `viewport` where they have a full specification on this tag.

The Web Application Tags

The next two tags, `apple-mobile-web-app-capable` and `apple-touch-fullscreen`, go together and should be set in conjunction with each other:

```
<meta name="apple-mobile-web-app-capable" content="no" />
<meta name="apple-touch-fullscreen" content="no" />
```

Typically you'll set both to **yes** or **no**, depending on your application. During your normal browsing within the browser, these tags do very little for you. They come into play once a user sets a shortcut on his or her home page while using an Apple device like an iPhone or iPad. When using such a shortcut, and if you have these tags set to **yes**, your webpage will run in a web application mode. All of the browser bling like the address bar and back buttons will disappear and your app will take up the entire screen, just like a native app (sweet!).

> *Why are there two of these tags? You could probably get away with just setting the "apple-mobile-web-app-capable" tag for iOS devices, since that is the only one documented on the Apple Developer site. The apple-touch-fullscreen appears to be from an earlier version of the framework. It's probably not needed in most cases, but it doesn't hurt anything to include it.*

Closely related to the `apple-mobile-web-app-capable` tag is the `apple-mobile-web-app-status-bar-style` tag. If you set `apple-mobile-web-app-capable` to **yes**, you can change the color of the status bar.

```
<meta name="apple-mobile-web-app-status-bar-style" content="black" />
```

You can set that tag to **default** (which turns it to gray), **black**, or **black-translucent**. This tag is totally optional and you don't see it used very often.

> *Warning: If you choose black-translucent, the header will bleed over on top of your normal jQuery.Mobile header bar, so you will have to account for that by putting 20 pixels of dead space in*

By setting these two simple values, you've made a webpage that looks and functions almost like a native application. You are still running a webpage and running a browser, but all of the things that make it look like a browser are hidden.

Use Caution When Using Web App Mode

When you first see these tags, you may be tempted to use them all the time on all of your sites—after all, they make your webpage look like a native app without any of the problems of creating a native app. However, there are a few gotchas to be aware of when using web app mode. The biggest problem comes when you try to link to an external item like a PDF file or an external website. When you do that, the link will open up in the Safari browser, so users will see a new window open and will lose their context in the app. Worse yet, when users return to your app, it will start all over at the beginning: splash screen, login, home page, etc. You won't notice this behavior when you test this in Safari on your desktop, but it will definitely be noticeable on a mobile device. Make sure you've tested all of your links before you commit to using this tag in your app.

Creating a Nice Icon on Your Desktop

As a web developer, you have probably used this tag before to create icons in the browser for your desktop websites:

```
<link rel="shortcut icon" href="~/favicon.ico" type="image/x-icon" />
<link rel="icon" href="~/favicon.ico" type="image/x-icon" />
```

You use the **icon** tags to have your browser shortcuts, tab bar, and header use your icon. Creating a good **favicon.ico** file has been kind of tricky in the past, but Microsoft has a really nice website to help you create one. Go to http://www.xiconeditor.com/ where you can easily upload any image (preferably 64 × 64 pixels), and the editor will create a perfectly formatted favicon.ico file for you. When you are done, you can save the file and place it in the root of your website.

Even though the **icon** tags work great on a desktop, they don't have the same effect on mobile devices. The following tag is essentially the mobile browser equivalent to the shortcut icon tag:

```
<link rel="apple-touch-icon" href="~/Content/images/apple-touch-
```

```
icon.png"/>
```

This tag will allow users to create a shortcut and have your pretty icon displayed as their desktop shortcut to your app. If you don't supply this tag, when users create a desktop shortcut, iOS devices will take a thumbnail snapshot of the app screen and use that. Android devices will use the system-defined bookmark icon.

At first glance, this tag seems simple, but there are many permutations of this tag that you will need to use. It works okay in most instances, but won't give you optimal results with the basic version. On an iOS device, using the basic version of this tag will add the highlight shadow on the upper half of your image. If you don't want to have that white shadow on your image, you can remove it by using a slightly modified tag (adding **-precomposed** to the name):

```
<link rel="apple-touch-icon-precomposed"
  href="~/Content/images/apple-touch-icon.png"/>
```

The deceptive part of this tag is that each of the mobile operating systems has its own specification for how big an icon *should* be. This tag supports an attribute that specifies different icons for different sizes.

Start by saving copies of your application icon image in each of the following sizes, putting them in your **Content/Images** folder, and using a naming scheme like this:

```
apple-touch-icon-57x57.png
apple-touch-icon-72x72.png
apple-touch-icon-114x114.png
apple-touch-icon-144x144.png
```

apple-touch-icon-57x57.png   apple-touch-icon-72x72.png   apple-touch-icon-114x114.png   apple-touch-icon-144x144.png

Multiple Sizes of Icons

The phone and the tablet use different sizes of icons, so we'll have to add unique lines to each of the layout files. Add the following tags to your **_Layout.Phone.cshtml** file:

```
<!-- iPhone Low-Res -->
<link rel="apple-touch-icon-precomposed" sizes="57x57"
  href="~/Content/images/apple-touch-icon-57x57.png" />
<!-- iPhone Hi-Res -->
<link rel="apple-touch-icon-precomposed" sizes="114x114"
  href="~/Content/images/apple-touch-icon-114x114.png" />
<!-- Android -->
<link rel="apple-touch-icon-precomposed" sizes="android-only"
  href="~/Content/images/apple-touch-icon-57x57.png" />
<!-- default -->
<link rel="apple-touch-icon-precomposed"
  href="~/Content/images/apple-touch-icon-57x57.png" />
```

The Android browser doesn't support the `size` tag so we will put in a value of `android-only` in one tag so that other browsers don't try to use this one. iOS versions before 4.2 don't support the `size` tag either, so they will use the last one specified in the list, which is why you see a default version without a size listed at the end of the code.

Do the same thing in your **_Layout.Tablet.cshtml** file by adding the following code (note that these tags are similar to but different than what we used in the **_Layout.Phone** page):

```
<!-- iPad Low-Res -->
<link rel="apple-touch-icon-precomposed" sizes="72x72"
  href="~/Content/images/apple-touch-icon-72x72.png" />
<!-- iPad Hi-Res -->
<link rel="apple-touch-icon-precomposed" sizes="144x144"
  href="~/Content/images/apple-touch-icon-144x144.png" />
<!-- Android -->
<link rel="apple-touch-icon-precomposed" sizes="android-only"
  href="~/Content/images/apple-touch-icon-57x57.png" />
<!-- default -->
<link rel="apple-touch-icon-precomposed"
  href="~/Content/images/apple-touch-icon-57x57.png" />
```

With these settings, you should be able to create shortcuts on a variety of iOS and Android devices and have a properly formatted and sized icon show up on the desktop.

Prompting the User to Create a Shortcut

Even though we now have the properly formatted HTML to create nice desktop shortcuts and icons, that does not mean that users will actually take the time to create the shortcut—it doesn't happen automatically! Let's look at a way that we can prompt users to create a desktop shortcut the first time they start our app. When using an iOS device, the `navigator.standalone` property will tell us whether a page is operating in full screen mode.

Here is some JavaScript we can use to perform this check. Save this JavaScript in the **/Scripts/PromptForBookmark.js** file:

```javascript
// Contents of file "/Scripts/PromptForBookmark.js"
$(document).ready(function () {
  // This script should only be enabled if you are using the
  // apple-mobile-web-app-capable=yes option.
  var cookie_name = "PromptForBookmarkCookie";
  var cookie_exists = false;
  documentCookies = document.cookie;
  if (documentCookies.length > 0) {
    cookie_exists = (documentCookies.indexOf(cookie_name + "=")
    != -1);
  }
  if (cookie_exists == false) {
    // If it's an iOS device, then we check if we are in a
    // full-screen mode, otherwise just move on.
    if ((navigator.userAgent.indexOf("iPhone") > 0 ||
        navigator.userAgent.indexOf("iPad") > 0 ||
        navigator.userAgent.indexOf("iPod") > 0)) {
      if (!navigator.standalone) {
        window.alert('This app is designed to be used in full screen mode.
For best results, click on the Create Bookmark icon in your toolbar and
select the Add to Home Screen option and start this app from the resulting
icon.');
      }
    }
    //Now that we've warned the user, set a cookie so that
    //the user won't be asked again.
    document.cookie = cookie_name +
      "=Told You So;expires=Monday, 31-Dec-2029 05:00:00 GMT";
  }
});
```

This script checks to see if the user has already been warned by checking for the existence of a cookie. If the user has not been warned before, the script will first make sure this is an iOS device by looking at the user agent, and then it will open an alert to notify the user that he or she should really use a desktop shortcut to start this application. Finally, it will store a cookie with a long expiration date so that the user won't be bothered by this again.

To enable this feature, enable the `apple-mobile-web-app-capable` option, and then add the following script line in your **_Layout.Phone.cshtml** and **_Layout.Tablet.cshtml** files:

```
<meta name="apple-touch-fullscreen" content="yes" />
<meta name="apple-mobile-web-app-capable" content="yes" />
<script type="text/javascript"
  src="@Url.Content("~/Scripts/PromptForBookmark.js")" ></script>
```

These tags will tell iOS devices to run the application in full-screen mode. They will also enable the script that informs the user that he or she should create a shortcut for this application the first time the application is run.

Creating a Splash Screen

Most applications show a nice-looking startup screen while you are loading the application. If you want to have a nice splash screen when the application is run in full-screen mode, you will need to add the following tag:

```
<link rel="apple-touch-startup-image" href="startup.png">
```

At first glance, this tag also seems simple, but once again, looks can be deceiving. In this first very simple example, this tag specifies the startup image that will be displayed when you start your app from a desktop shortcut and you have it set to use the web app mode. Unfortunately, most of the time this tag will have no effect at all. Your image needs to be EXACTLY the right size for your specific device, so there are many possible options. If the conditions are not exactly right, then the image just doesn't show up. You can even have the image just right in portrait mode, and then if the user changes the device to landscape mode, the image will not appear.

To make things even more complicated, there are two versions of displays you have to worry about: the original iPhone and iPad, and the newer Retina displays for the iPhone and iPad. The following table lists the sizes for the startup image:

Device	Resolution	Portrait Startup Size	Landscape Startup Size
iPhone – Original	320 x 480	320 x 460	480 x 300
iPhone – Retina	640 x 960	640 x 920	960 x 600
iPad – Original	1024 x 768	768 x 1004	1024 x 724
iPad – Retina	2048 x 1536	1536 x 2008	2048 x 1496

As you can see from the chart, on the original devices we have to subtract 20 pixels from one side to account for the header bar, and on the Retina devices we have to subtract 40 pixels. You may want to make your images different sizes, but don't give in to that temptation. These devices are very fussy and if you don't make your images EXACTLY one of these sizes they simply won't show up. To account for all of these possible situations, you will need to create each of the following images and put them in your **Content\Images** folder:

```
startup_image_320x460.png (iPhone Low-Res)
startup_image_640x920.png (iPhone Retina)
```

```
startup_image_480x300.png (iPhone Low-Res Landscape)
startup_image_960x600.png (iPhone Retina Landscape)

startup_image_768x1004.png (iPad Low-Res)
startup_image_1536x2008.png (iPad Retina)

startup_image_1024x748.png (iPad Low-Res Landscape)
startup_image_2048x1496.png (iPad Retina Landscape)
```

> *You can name them whatever you want, but these names are what are used in the HTML samples that follow.*

In order to get your images to show up on all the different devices at the right times, you'll need a variety of different versions of the `apple-touch-startup-image` tags in your page. Adding CSS media rules will help to determine which image to use in each situation.

The best place to put this code is in your layout pages. Add the following tags to your **_Layout.Phone.cshtml**:

```
<!-- iPhone Low-Res -->
<link rel="apple-touch-startup-image"
  href="~/Content/images/startup_image_320x460.png"
  media="(device-width: 320px)" />
<!-- iPhone Retina -->
<link rel="apple-touch-startup-image"
  href="~/Content/images/startup_image_640x920.png"
  media="(device-width: 640px) and
  (-webkit-device-pixel-ratio: 2)" />
<!-- iPhone Low-Res Landscape -->
<link rel="apple-touch-startup-image"
  href="~/Content/images/startup_image_480x300.png"
  media="(device-width: 320px) and (orientation: landscape)" />
<!-- iPhone Retina Landscape -->
<link rel="apple-touch-startup-image"
  href="~/Content/images/startup_image_960x600.png"
  media="(device-width: 640px) and (orientation: landscape) and
  (-webkit-device-pixel-ratio: 2)" />
<!-- (iPhone default) -->
<link rel="apple-touch-startup-image"
  href="~/Content/images/startup_image_320x460.png" />
```

Do the same thing for your tablet layout pages by creating the following tags (note that once again these are similar to but different than the tags we used in the phone pages):

```
<!-- iPad Low-Res -->
<link rel="apple-touch-startup-image"
  href="~/Content/images/startup_image_768x1004.png"
```

```
  media="(device-width: 768px) and (orientation: portrait)" />
<!-- iPad Retina -->
<link rel="apple-touch-startup-image"
  href="~/Content/images/startup_image_1536x2008.png"
  media="(device-width: 1536px) and (orientation: portrait)
  and (-webkit-device-pixel-ratio: 2)" />
<!-- iPad Low-Res Landscape -->
<link rel="apple-touch-startup-image"
  href="~/Content/images/startup_image_1024x748.png"
  media="(device-width: 768px) and (orientation: landscape)" />
<!-- iPad Retina Landscape -->
<link rel="apple-touch-startup-image"
  href="~/Content/images/startup_image_2048x1496.png"
  media="(device-width: 1536px) and (orientation: landscape)
  and (-webkit-device-pixel-ratio: 2)" />
<!-- (iPad default) -->
<link rel="apple-touch-startup-image"
  href="~/Content/images/startup_image_768x1004.png" />
```

With these tags in place, you *should* have a startup image that will display for all of the iOS devices currently on the market. Although you can use the web app mode and create desktop icons on an Android device, these startup images will be ignored on Android devices.

> *Note: I still have not been able to get the startup image to work perfectly on the new iPad Retina display when it is in landscape mode. The image does display, but shows up in the lower quarter of the screen with the other three quarters of the screen showing up white. I'm hoping that this is a bug that will be addressed in a future update.*

Chapter 8   Tips and Tricks

"Do not try and bend the spoon. That's impossible. Instead...only try to realize the truth. There is no spoon. Then you'll see that it is not the spoon that bends, it is only yourself."
   Young boy in *The Matrix*

Using Partial Views to Minimize Duplication

One of the major problems with the type of website that we have been creating so far is that we are replicating pages in our site, and with that comes the curse of duplicate content. One way you can avoid replicating your content is by creating partial views that you share between the different device pages. The following three screenshots are the exact same URL with the exact same content, but each is organized and optimized for the platform it is targeting, and each shares the same content file.

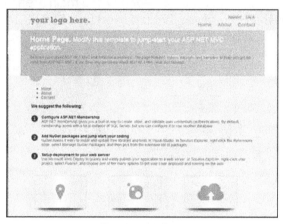

Desktop View

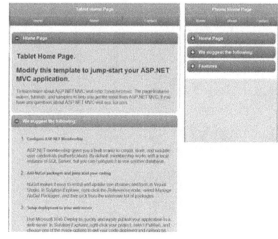

Tablet and Phone Views

Let's look at the source code for each of these pages, starting with the desktop view:

```
@{ ViewBag.Title = "Home Page"; }
@section featured {
  @Html.Partial("_Index_SubPage1")
}
<ul >
  @Html.Partial("_Index_SubPage2")
</ul>
<h3>We suggest the following:</h3>
@Html.Partial("_Index_SubPage3")
<section class="features">
  @Html.Partial("_Index_SubPage4")
</section>
```

That's it—that's the entire page. For each of the main areas on the page, you can see that the content has been moved to a partial view file, so there is very little left on the actual page.

Let's start by creating the mobile views with a very similar layout. Here is the phone page:

```
@{ Layout = "../Shared/_Layout.Phone.cshtml"; }
@{ ViewBag.Title = "Phone Home Page"; }

<h2>Home Page</h2>
@Html.Partial("_Index_SubPage1")

@* -- Moved to the Shared/_Layout.Phone.cshtml *@
@*    @Html.Partial("_Index_SubPage2")*@

<h2>We suggest the following:</h2>
@Html.Partial("_Index_SubPage3")

<h2>Features</h2>
@Html.Partial("_Index_SubPage4")
```

And here is the tablet page:

```
@{ Layout = "../Shared/_Layout.Tablet.cshtml"; }
@{ ViewBag.Title = "Tablet Home Page"; }
<h2>Home Page</h2>
@Html.Partial("_Index_SubPage1")

@* -- Moved to the Shared/_Layout.Tablet.cshtml *@
@*    @Html.Partial("_Index_SubPage2")*@

<h2>We suggest the following:</h2>
@Html.Partial("_Index_SubPage3")

<h2>Features</h2>
@Html.Partial("_Index_SubPage4")
```

Note that we removed the **_Index_SubPage2** because that is the menu that we already have in the base layout page. This code won't produce the sleek page shown in the previous screenshot quite yet, but it will have all of the content on the page. We'll look at adding the collapsible containers in just a minute.

Using this type of coding pattern raises your chances of success tremendously because you can optimize the design of your pages to match the device, but at the same time save yourself from having to maintain content in three different places at once. With this model, when you change the content in one place, it's changed on all three platforms at the same time!

Collapsible Containers and Reusable Content

Let's go back to the collapsible containers we referenced briefly in Chapter 3. jQuery.Mobile makes it very easy to create these. Let's look at an example of this in action.

Let's modify the mobile views we just created to put the partial view content inside of a `div` with a role of `collapsible`. If you use that type of `div` container and you have to add a header tag at the top of your content, you'll end up with a nice-looking bar with a plus or minus sign at the top of the container. You can see that we've set the phone containers to be collapsed and the tablet containers to be expanded by default since we have different device specifications.

Here is the finished code for the phone page:

```
@{ Layout = "../Shared/_Layout.Phone.cshtml"; }
@{ ViewBag.Title = "Phone Home Page"; }

<div data-role="collapsible" data-theme="b" data-content-theme="b"
  data-collapsed="true">
  <h2>Home Page</h2>
  @Html.Partial("_Index_SubPage1")
</div>

@* -- Moved to the Shared/_Layout.Phone.cshtml *@
@*    @Html.Partial("_Index_SubPage2")*@

<div data-role="collapsible" data-theme="b"
  data-content-theme="b" data-collapsed="true">
  <h2>We suggest the following:</h2>
  @Html.Partial("_Index_SubPage3")
</div>

<div data-role="collapsible" data-theme="b"
  data-content-theme="b" data-collapsed="true">
  <h2>Features</h2>
  @Html.Partial("_Index_SubPage4")
</div>
```

And here is the code for the finished tablet page:

```
@{ Layout = "../Shared/_Layout.Tablet.cshtml"; }
@{ ViewBag.Title = "Tablet Home Page"; }
<div data-role="collapsible" data-theme="b"
  data-content-theme="b" data-collapsed="false">
  <h2>Home Page</h2>
  @Html.Partial("_Index_SubPage1")
```

```
</div>

@* -- Moved to the Shared/_Layout.Tablet.cshtml *@
@*      @Html.Partial("_Index_SubPage2")*@

<div data-role="collapsible" data-theme="b"
  data-content-theme="b" data-collapsed="false">
  <h2>We suggest the following:</h2>
  @Html.Partial("_Index_SubPage3")
</div>

<div data-role="collapsible" data-theme="b"
  data-content-theme="b" data-collapsed="false">
  <h2>Features</h2>
  @Html.Partial("_Index_SubPage4")
</div>
```

This source code will now produce pages that look like the screenshots at the beginning of the chapter. With this code, you now have three pages that look distinctly different and behave differently, but they all share the exact same URL and content. The only difference is in the device that requests the page.

Desktop/Mobile ViewSwitcher

MVC 4 has a new feature available called browser overriding, which lets users override their normal user agent string and view your page as if they were using a different browser. Using this, you can allow users to come to your site on their phone and get your mobile optimized view, and then they can request to see what it would look like on a desktop or a tablet.

> *Note: This feature only affects the views and layouts in MVC, and doesn't affect any other ASP.NET feature that looks at the Request.Browser object.*

There are several options available to you for this feature. There is actually a NuGet package that you can download to enable this, but the following code has been customized to work with the mobile framework concepts that we have been developing in this book.

There are two components that you need to enable this feature: a view and the corresponding controller. Let's look at the view first:

```
<span style="font-size: 0.7em;">
Switch To:
@Html.ActionLink("Desktop View", "SwitchView", "ViewSwitcher",
  new { mobile = false, mobileType = "Desktop",
  returnUrl = Request.Url.PathAndQuery },
  new { rel = "external" })
@Html.ActionLink("Tablet View", "SwitchView", "ViewSwitcher",
  new { mobile = true, mobileType = "Tablet",
  returnUrl = Request.Url.PathAndQuery },
  new { rel = "external" })
@Html.ActionLink("Phone View", "SwitchView", "ViewSwitcher",
  new { mobile = true, mobileType = "Phone",
  returnUrl = Request.Url.PathAndQuery },
  new { rel = "external" })
@Html.ActionLink("Default View", "SwitchView", "ViewSwitcher",
  new { mobile = false, mobileType = "Default",
  returnUrl = Request.Url.PathAndQuery },
  new { rel = "external" })
</span>
```

Switch To: Desktop View   Tablet View   Phone View   Default View

View Options

So far, we have been working to develop three distinct views for our site: a desktop, tablet, and phone version. The links shown in the previous screenshot let users choose any of the three display options, or reset to the default view that their device would normally request.

The controller that catches this link and processes it looks like this:

```csharp
using System.Web.Mvc;
using System.Web.WebPages;

namespace Demo.Controllers
{
  public class ViewSwitcherController : Controller
  {
    public RedirectResult SwitchView(bool mobile, string mobileType,
      string returnUrl)
    {
      mobileType = (mobileType == null) ?
        string.Empty : mobileType.Trim().ToLower();
      if (mobileType == "default")
      {
        HttpContext.ClearOverriddenBrowser();
      }
      else
      {
        if (mobileType == string.Empty) mobileType = "mobile";
        switch (mobileType)
        {
          case "desktop":
            HttpContext.SetOverriddenBrowser("Mozilla/5.0 (Macintosh; U;
Intel Mac OS X 10_6_8; en-us) AppleWebKit/534.55.3 (KHTML, like Gecko)
Version/5.1.5 Safari/534.55.3");
            break;
          case "tablet":
          case "ipad":
            HttpContext.SetOverriddenBrowser("Mozilla/5.0 (iPad; U; CPU OS
4_3_3 like Mac OS X; en-us) AppleWebKit/533.17.9 (KHTML, like Gecko)
Version/5.0.2 Mobile/8J2 Safari/6533.18.5");
            break;
          case "phone":
          case "iphone":
            HttpContext.SetOverriddenBrowser("Mozilla/5.0 (iPhone; U; CPU
iPhone OS 4_3_3 like Mac OS X; en-us) AppleWebKit/533.17.9 (KHTML, like
Gecko) Version/5.0.2 Mobile/8J2 Safari/6533.18.5");
            break;
          default:
            HttpContext.SetOverriddenBrowser(BrowserOverride.Mobile);
            break;
        }
      }
      return Redirect(returnUrl);
    }
  }
}
```

The new functions provided by MVC 4 that this controller uses are **SetOverriddenBrowser** and **ClearOverriddenBrowser**. In this case, if a user requests a desktop view, the user agent is set to simulate a

Macintosh desktop, but you can easily set it to whatever user agent you want. In our framework, it really doesn't make much difference what desktop user agent you specify as any of them will return the default desktop view.

With this code in place, all you have to do is to add the following line into your layout pages to include the `ViewSwitcher` code:

```
@Html.Partial("_ViewSwitcher")
```

Some designers believe this should be at the top of the page above your mobile view, and others like to put it at the bottom, but it's really a matter of personal preference where you display these links.

Having this link gives your users a degree of control that they didn't have before by letting them use the desktop site if the mobile pages are not functioning properly for some reason.

HTML 5 Tags

There are a variety of new HTML 5 tags that can be very useful on a mobile device. You can specify HTML 5 tags in your app by setting the `<input type=` parameter. These tags include (but are not limited to): `email`, `tel`, `url`, `number`, `search`, `time`, `date`, `month`, `datetime`, and `datetime-local`. Many of these have very limited support on mobile browsers (especially on Android browsers), and there are some, such as `week` and `color`, that don't work at all on certain mobile platforms like iOS, and others that work on current versions of iOS (5.x) but not earlier versions (4.x). We'll discuss a few of them here and see how you can easily use these in your MVC project.

Editor Templates

Here is an example of the HTML that would create a **Phone** field:

```
<input class="text-box single-line" name="Phone" type="tel" value="" />
```

This code will generate a screen on an iOS phone that looks like this:

Phone Screen

Notice that the standard keyboard has been replaced with one that consists of only numbers which gives the user much larger buttons and a greater chance of entering the proper information. In a similar fashion, the `email` and `url` attributes will display a keyboard that has letters and common web address characters like the @ sign, which doesn't appear on the default keyboard for normal text fields.

Remember what I said in Chapter 4 about some things not

working when you are using Safari as a mobile emulator? The email and url tags (as well as some others) are one of those things. These special keyboards won't pop up in the desktop version of Safari.

Also, most of the number and date picker tags in this section do not work on Android devices at this time.

You can manually create the HTML to put in that special `input type` attribute, but in MVC there is a much better way to do this: data annotations. Let's start by modifying a model definition:

```
public class SampleModel
{
  // -- Other fields omitted here for brevity.
  [DataType(DataType.PhoneNumber)]
  [Display(Name = "Phone", Prompt = "Phone:")]
  public string Phone { get; set; }
}
```

When we add the `DataType` annotation, this will tell MVC that this is a special type of string, and it will be treated differently when composing a view. However, if all you do is add this data annotation, you won't see anything different; you need one more piece to this puzzle: editor templates.

These templates are not supplied with the standard MVC project template, so you must go get them yourself and add them to your project. These templates must reside in a folder named **EditorTemplates** under the **Shared** folder. The templates can be found by fetching a NuGet package (`Install-Package MvcHtml5Templates`).

In our model definition, we've specified that our **Phone** field has a `DataType` of `PhoneNumber`, so MVC will look for and use the **PhoneNumber** template when creating the HTML for editing this field. The **PhoneNumber.cshtml** file is very simple, and contains only the following code:

```
@Html.TextBox("", ViewData.TemplateInfo.FormattedModelValue,
  new { @class = "text-box single-line", type = "tel" })
```

In your view file, all you need to do is use the `EditorFor` helper on your field and it will automatically generate the updated HTML now. (Note that if you use the `TextBoxFor` helper without any special parameters, it won't work automatically.)

```
@Html.EditorFor(m => m.Phone)
```

This combination of model data annotation, editor templates, and the `EditorFor` helper will generate the code that we started with earlier. MVC does all the hard stuff for us—pretty sweet, huh?

```
<input class="text-box single-line" name="Phone" type="tel" value="" />
```

Let's look at another example: the `DateTime` helper. Let's edit our model again and add a `DateTime` field:

```
public class SampleModel
{
    // -- Other fields omitted here.
    [DataType(DataType.DateTime)]
    public DateTime ContactDateTime { get; set; }
}
```

Next we'll add a **DateTime.cshtml** editor template in the **Shared** folder:

```
@Html.TextBox("", ViewData.TemplateInfo.FormattedModelValue,
    new { @class = "text-box single-line", type = "datetime" })
```

While we're at it, let's create a **Month.cshtml** editor template too:

```
@Html.TextBox("", ViewData.TemplateInfo.FormattedModelValue,
    new { @class = "text-box single-line", type = "month" })
```

After adding this field to our view, we can use any of the following `EditorFor` statements:

```
@Html.EditorFor(m => m.ContactDateTime)
@Html.EditorFor(m => m.ContactDateTime, "DateTime")
@Html.EditorFor(m => m.ContactDateTime, "Month")
```

When you run this code on an iOS phone, you will get one of these editors:

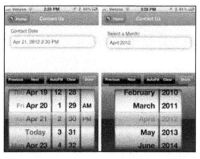

Date Pickers in iOS

It looks like a native app and behaves like a native app, but it's all HTML!

If you want to get this to work on all mobile platforms right now, you will have to try using a third-party tool like Mobiscroll which can be found at http://mobiscroll.com/.

On your desktop, you won't notice any difference yet. If you want a nice date picker on your desktop, you will need to install the jQuery.UI components if they are not already in your project. If you have already added the **DateType.Date** data annotation in your model, and you have included the **Date.cshtml** editor template, then there are only a few small changes that you need to make. In your **_Layout.cshtml** page (or in your desktop bundles in the **Global.asax** if you are using minification), you will need to include the **jquery-ui.min.js** and the **jquery-ui.min.css** files, and you will need to add the following script in the header of the **_Layout** file to enable the fields:

```
<script type="text/javascript">
  $(document).ready(function () {
    $('.date').datepicker({ dateFormat: "mm/dd/yy" });
  });
</script>
```

That's it—now you will have a nice fancy date picker pop-up in your application that looks like this (with almost no work on your part!):

Date Picker

Before you commit to using these features, you should make sure they are supported on the devices that you want to target. A couple of good resources to check are:

- http://mobilehtml5.org/: This site lists many HTML 5 features and which browsers and operating systems support them.

- http://www.quirksmode.org/html5/inputs_mobile.html: This site lists some of the specific HTML tags and attributes (like the ones shown in this chapter), and details which mobile operating systems support those tags.

Search Fields

Another useful field type is the `search` type. If you want a field that looks like a search field, just add the **Search** template type on a string field. In the following code sample we don't have a `Search` data annotation that we can add to our model, so we'll tell the `EditorFor` helper to use a specific template:

```
@Html.EditorFor(m => m.SearchTxt, "Search")
```

The code in the Search Editor Template looks like this:

```
@Html.TextBox("", ViewData.TemplateInfo.FormattedModelValue,
   new { @class = "text-box single-line", type = "search" })
```

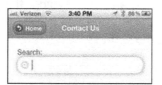

Search Field

Notice how the field corners are much more rounded than a normal text box, and how it has a magnifying glass inside the text field? These are just subtle hints to the user that this is a special field.

We won't go into all of the editor templates here because there are several with many options each. Some work with the `EditorFor` and data annotations, and some will need a little more manual tweaking.

Special HTML 5 Attributes

There are a few other special attributes that you will appreciate. The `Required` attribute is a nice HTML 5 attribute, but that should be handled by the `Required` data annotation in your model, so we won't address it here.

One attribute that is very useful is the `placeholder` attribute. This will place light gray text in the text box field to give users a hint of what to type, and then the text disappears when they click in the box. Let's go back and enhance our **Search** box by using the `TextBoxFor` helper so we can easily add an extra attribute. Remember that I mentioned the default `TextBoxFor` helper wouldn't use a template from the data annotation? You can specify one by editing the `HtmlAttributes`. Since that is how we need to specify the `placeholder` tag, we'll specify both the editor template and the `placeholder` attribute using the `TextBoxFor` command.

```
@Html.TextBoxFor(m => m.SearchTxt,
    new { type= "search", placeholder = "enter search terms" })
```

Placeholder in a Search Field

Now you've got the *enter search terms* placeholder text in your search field. When you click inside the field and start typing, the placeholder goes away. In addition, the user gets a nice little clear button on the right of the text box. Not bad for one simple little attribute!

Other attributes you may want to investigate adding to your text boxes are `autocorrect="off"`, `autocomplete="off"`, and `autocapitalize="off"`.

The MVC 4 Tilde Tidbit

Here is one awesome feature of MVC 4 that we have been using through all of the examples so far, but you may not have noticed. Take a look at this code:

```
<img src="~/Content/images/icon.png"/>
```

If you were coding in MVC 3, you would expect to see a tag like this:

```
<img src="@Url.Content("~/Content/images/icon.png")"/>
```

This is one of the small, overlooked features of MVC 4 that is really useful. If you look at the HTML that is generated, these two statements will both generate exactly the same HTML, but the first is much cleaner. It doesn't seem like much, but anything that makes your code more readable is a nice feature in my book.

Chapter 9   More jQuery.Mobile Features

"You know nothing for sure, except the fact that you know nothing for sure."
  John F. Kennedy

One thing I've learned over the years is that the more I learn, the more that I realize there is to learn. In this chapter, we'll look at some of the things that are important to know about jQuery.Mobile. There are other books that explore many of these concepts in more depth, and I would encourage you to read them if the concepts discussed here pique your interest. This chapter is intended to give you a good overview of some of the more important topics of jQuery.Mobile.

jQuery.Mobile Container Objects

In Chapter 6, we discussed the main jQuery.Mobile sections: `page`, `header`, `content`, `footer`, and `navbar`. There are many other sections available which we will briefly discuss here.

Nested Collapsible Containers

We talked about the collapsible container object in the Tips and Tricks section already, but one thing we didn't talk about was nesting containers. You can nest collapsible containers inside of other collapsible containers. However, using more than two levels is not recommended because of the complexity that ensues.

In addition to nesting, one other thing you can do with collapsible containers is create an accordion-type effect using the `data-role="collapsible-set"` attribute. If you wrap a set of collapsible containers inside this attribute, you get a nice, space-saving effect. Only one of the containers in the set will open at one time, so when you click on any of the plus signs, all of the other containers will automatically close.

```
<div data-role="collapsible-set">
  <div data-role="collapsible" data-collapsed="false">
    <h2>Section 1 Title</h2>
    Section 1 Content
  </div>
  <div data-role="collapsible" data-collapsed="false">
    <h2>Section 2 Title</h2>
    Section 2 Content
  </div>
  <div data-role="collapsible" data-collapsed="false">
    <h2>Section 3 Title</h2>
    Section 3 Content
  </div>
</div>
```

Here is an example with plain collapsible containers on the left and containers using the accordion effect on the right.

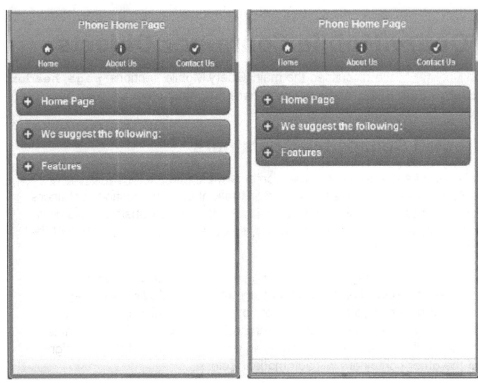

Plain Collapsible Containers (Left) and Containers with Accordion Effect (Right)

Field Container

If you are creating forms, you will probably want to wrap your fields inside a field container as done in the following code sample:

```
<div data-role="fieldcontain">
  @Html.LabelFor(m => m.UserName)
  @Html.TextBoxFor(m => m.UserName)<br />
  <span style="Color: Red;">@Html.ValidationMessageFor(m =>
    m.UserName)</span>
</div>
```

This tag helps mostly when you are working with wider screens. The framework will align the input and label side by side if the screen width is greater than 480 pixels, or it will stack them vertically if it is smaller than that. This tag will also add a thin bottom line below each of the fields to help break up the screen visually.

List View

You have probably used list components many times in your projects. jQuery.Mobile has many features that can enhance lists, and we could have an entire chapter just for that topic. However, we will cover only the most frequently used here, and will create a short cheat sheet of options that you will come back to often.

Simple Unordered List: Full Screen Width

```
<ul data-role="listview">
```

This example creates a simple unordered list that uses the full screen width.

Inset List

```
<ul data-role="listview" data-inset="true">
```

This example creates a simple unordered list that is in a bubble with rounded corners, and is inset from the borders a little bit.

Ordered List

```
<ol data-role="listview">
```

This example creates a simple ordered list with a number for each list item.

List with Search Header

```
<ul data-role="listview" data-filter="true">
```

This example creates an unordered list with a search bar at the top of the screen that will let users filter the contents of the list easily.

List Header or Divider

```
<li data-role="list-divider">@ViewBag.Title</li>
```

This example creates a header item in your list, which separates the content visually.

Simple List Item

```
<li>Home</li>
```

This example creates a simple list item.

Bold List Item

```
<li><h1>Home</h1></li>
```

This example creates an item which will appear much larger in the list. You can adjust the size by using different header level tags, or even use a <p> tag to decrease the size of the row.

List Item with Link

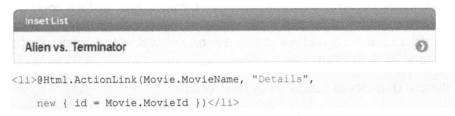

```
<li>@Html.ActionLink(Movie.MovieName, "Details",

    new { id = Movie.MovieId })</li>
```

This example creates an interactive list item. Users can click anywhere in the row to activate the link.

List Item with Link and Icon

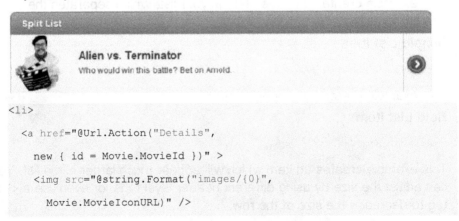

```
<li>

  <a href="@Url.Action("Details",

    new { id = Movie.MovieId })" >

    <img src="@string.Format("images/{0}.png",

      Movie.Genre)"

    alt="Email" class="ui-li-icon" />@Movie.MovieName</a>

</li>
```

This example creates an item with an icon on the left that is part of the clickable area for this item. You can specify any icon you want or make it data driven.

Complex Split Button List Item

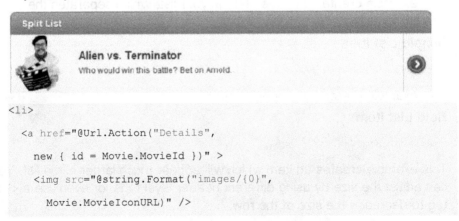

```
<li>

  <a href="@Url.Action("Details",

    new { id = Movie.MovieId })" >

    <img src="@string.Format("images/{0}",

      Movie.MovieIconURL)" />
```

```
    <h3>@Movie.MovieName</h3>

    <p>@Movie.MovieDscr</p>

  </a>

  <a href="@Url.Action("Purchase",
    new { id = Movie.MovieId })">Purchase Movie</a>

</li>
```

This example creates a moderately complicated split-button view. The first link controls the left portion of the item, and encompasses an icon, title, and description. The second link automatically creates a small section on the right with an icon and ignores any text you put in there. A bordered arrow icon is used as the default, but you can specify any of the jQuery.Mobile icons by putting the **data-split-icon** tag on the **<ul>** tag at the top of the section that defines your list.

List Item with Count Bubble

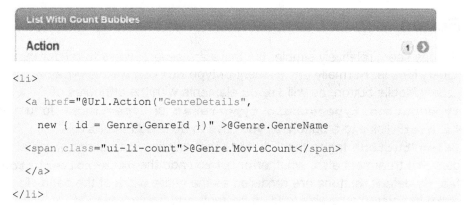

```
<li>

  <a href="@Url.Action("GenreDetails",

    new { id = Genre.GenreId })" >@Genre.GenreName

  <span class="ui-li-count">@Genre.MovieCount</span>

  </a>

</li>
```

This tag creates a list item with a count bubble number on the right. Typically this will show you the number of items you would expect to see if you clicked on this row. In this particular example, we're showing the number of movies in a single genre.

Columns

jQuery.Mobile offers a convenient way to lay out the screen with a grid-based system of two, three, four, or five columns. However, as we discussed in previous chapters, try to think about mobile devices in more of a single column format (or two columns), so don't get carried away with this and return to the table-driven HTML design mentality of years past! There is a place for tables, such as when trying to put a few items side by side, especially when they are in a container like a footer, but use restraint. Here is an example of a simple two column grid:

```
<div class="ui-grid-a">
   <div class="ui-block-a"><strong>I'm Block A</strong>
     and text inside will wrap</div>
   <div class="ui-block-b"><strong>I'm Block B</strong>
     and text inside will wrap</div>
</div>
```

The class name will determine how many columns are created. In this case, we've used the `ui-grid-a` class, which signifies that we want two columns, and those columns are labeled `ui-block-a` and `ui-block-b`. If you want three columns, use the `ui-grid-b` tag and add a `ui-block-c div`. For four columns, use the `ui-grid-c` tag and add a `ui-block-d div`. And finally, for five columns, use the `ui-grid-d` tag and add a `ui-block-e div`; however, for most screens you'll probably be better off just avoiding this one.

Button

Buttons seem relatively simple, but there are several ways to render them in jQuery.Mobile. Normally any element of type `button` will render as a jQuery.Mobile button, as will `input` elements with the attributes of `type=button`, `type=submit`, `type=reset`, or `type=image`. To turn any `<a href>` link into a button, all you have to do is add the `data-role="button"` tag to that link. Note that any link in a header or footer gets that treatment also, whether or not you add the `data-role=button` tag. By default, buttons are rendered as the entire width of the page. To make the button auto-size to fit its content, add the tag `data-inline="true"` to the button. As we mentioned in previous chapters, you can also add icons to the button using the `data-icon` attribute, and you can set the position of that icon using the `data-iconpos` attribute.

If you want to group several buttons together into one compact container, you can use the `controlgroup` container. By default, the container lists the buttons vertically, but you can change that by setting the `data-type` attribute. Starting with jQuery.Mobile version 1.1, you can also add the `data-mini` attribute so that your buttons are rendered in a smaller format.

Control Group

```
<div data-role="controlgroup" data-type="horizontal"
  data-mini="true">
  <a href="index.html" data-role="button">Yes</a>
  <a href="index.html" data-role="button">No</a>
  <a href="index.html" data-role="button">Maybe</a>
</div>
```

Dialogs

jQuery.Mobile supports a pop-up dialog item which operates in a modal fashion (i.e. you have to close the dialog before you move on to something else). You will want to use these when asking for confirmation from a user ("Are you sure want to delete this?"), requiring the user to choose between a couple of choices ("Black or Blue?"), or giving the user information ("Your order has been submitted!").

A dialog is very simple to create. Just create your page as a view like any other view, and then when you link to that view, add the **data-rel="dialog"** tag to the link as shown in the following code sample:

```
<a href="@Url.Action("Delete", new { id = Movie.MovieId })"
  data-rel="dialog">Delete @Movie.MovieName</a>
```

You can also add the **data-role="dialog"** tag in your page instead of using the **data-role="page"** tag, and then you won't have to include it on every link referencing your page. In our case, since we are using shared layout pages, that means you would set up a **LayoutDialog.Phone.cshtml** file and a **LayoutDialog.Tablet.cshtml** file.

When a user clicks on a link in the dialog page, the dialog page is automatically closed and the link is opened. If you want to go back to the previous page, just include the **data-rel="back"** attribute on the link.

NoJS

jQuery.Mobile rates its browser support on a scale from A to C, with A meaning full support, B meaning full support minus AJAX, and C meaning support for basic HTML only. If you want to provide content for browsers that are not A-grade supported, you can add a special section that is just for them as shown in the following code sample:

```
<div data-role="nojs">
  Please upgrade your phone!
</div>
```

Multipage Documents

All of the examples we've seen so far in our MVC projects have used single-page templates. In other words, there is one and only one `<div data-role="page">` element on a page. jQuery.Mobile supports the concept of a multipage document in which you can define multiple `<div data-role="page">` elements, each with a different page. Each page element must have a unique ID such as `<div id="divExample">`. When you switch pages, you must specify a link with that ID `<a href="#divExample">`, which will cause the browser to look for that internal page and then transition it into view.

This idea is very attractive because it makes your site extremely fast when switching between pages. However, one drawback is that if you make your home page a multipage document with all of your pages on it, your entire site is loaded the first time a user hits the page, including all of the images and content on all of the sub-pages. This can make your page very slow to load, and it also makes it hard to track any sort of website analytics on a page-level basis.

In addition, if you start on a single-page document and then link to a multipage document, you must use the `data-ajax="false"` attribute on the link. If you don't, the framework will only load the first page node when it does an AJAX request.

If you are considering using multipage documents, make sure you test it thoroughly on actual devices. Mixing that with `"apple-mobile-web-app-capable"` tags can cause a lot of frustration when debugging your app.

> *I have developed full sites using multipage documents, but have converted some of them back to single-page sites. Some of those sites are still live with multipage design, but I'll probably switch those back over to single-page the next time I have to make a major change.*

Custom Icons

In a previous section we discussed how you can put icons on your buttons using the standard built-in icons. However, the selection is limited and it won't be long before you will find yourself saying, "I wish they had an icon that looked like an ice cream sandwich," or something equally absurd.

jQuery.Mobile makes it easy to create your own custom icons that you can use in your project. The standard jQuery.Mobile icons use a CSS sprite technique to combine all of their images into one image, and then display a portion of that image using a CSS style sheet tag. Take a look at the **/Content/Images/icons-36-white.png** file to see the file with all the standard icons.

You can create your own icons in a file similar to that one and then reference it the same way in your code. Let's look at an example. The following is an image file (displayed over a dark background) with five custom icons:

Custom Icon Sprite

Note the spacing in this sprite. It's got alternating sections of 36 pixels of content, and 36 pixels of transparent background, which make it cleaner and easier to use in CSS.

To use these custom icons, you will need to create the following CSS styles:

```
/* create multiple icons using a sprite with multiple images */
.ui-icon-custom-bell,
.ui-icon-custom-donot,
.ui-icon-custom-asterick,
.ui-icon-custom-thought,
.ui-icon-custom-bug {
  background-image: url(images/CustomIcons-36-white.png);
  -moz-background-size: 180px 18px;
  -o-background-size: 180px 18px;
  -webkit-background-size: 180px 18px;
  background-size: 180px 18px;
}

.ui-icon-custom-bell {
  background-position:   -0 50%;
}
.ui-icon-custom-donot {
  background-position:   -36px 50%;
}
.ui-icon-custom-asterick {
```

```css
  background-position:    -72px 50%;
}
.ui-icon-custom-thought {
  background-position:    -108px 50%;
}
.ui-icon-custom-bug {
  background-position:    -144px 50%;
}
/* Create an icon using a single image without sprites. */
.ui-icon-custom-bugimage {
  background-image: url(images/Bug18.png);
}
/* Hi-res version. */
@media only screen and (-webkit-min-device-pixel-ratio: 2)
{
  .ui-icon-custom-bugimage {
    background-image: url(images/Bug36.png) !important;
    background-size: 18px 18px;
  }
}
```

It may seem a bit counterintuitive that we show the background position as a negative number. What we are doing is telling our page to shift the image that many pixels to the left. In other words, for the **custom-thought** icon, we have the page chop off the first 108 pixels from the left side of the image and then show the result.

The last two styles demonstrate how you can reference a single image without using the sprite technique, and how you can target Retina displays with a high-resolution image by setting the `pixel-ratio` attribute to 2 when you are using a high-resolution Apple screen.

This style sheet should be saved and referenced in your layout pages. You can embed these style tags in your page if you want, but I'd recommend creating a site-specific style sheet. By default, MVC creates a **Site.css** file in your **Content** folder. A best practice is to create a **Site.Mobile.css** file in the **Content** folder and put your custom mobile styles there, then include that style sheet in each of your mobile layout pages (or in your custom mobile bundle if you are using that technique).

Now that we have our image created and our style sheets that define the tags, we can now reference these new icon tags in our page just like we reference the standard icons. The first item in the following code sample uses a stock icon, the second uses a custom sprite icon, and the third uses a custom image.

```html
<div data-role="navbar" data-theme="b" data-iconpos="top">
  <ul>
    <li>@Html.ActionLink("Home", "Index", "Home", null,
      new { data_icon = "home" })</li>
```

```
    <li>@Html.ActionLink("About Us", "About", "Home", null,
       new { data_icon = "custom-thought" })</li>
    <li>@Html.ActionLink("Bug Us", "Contact", "Home", null,
       new { data_icon = "custom-bugimage" })</li>
  </ul>
</div>
```

Header with Stock and Custom Icons

Now that you know how to create your own icon files and use them, you are limited only by your imagination. Get your graphic designer to draw some custom images for you and make your site look unique!

The example images and Photoshop file used to create the sprite are included in the sample code file. Enjoy!

Mini UI Elements

One of the nifty new features in jQuery.Mobile 1.1 is the ability to create mini-elements. All of the form elements accept a new `data-mini="true"` tag. You can also put this tag on the `controlgroup` for making a group of buttons smaller. This tag has no effect on the elements other than to make them smaller, but can be very useful if you are trying to put multiple items into a header or footer.

jQuery.Mobile Startup Options

There are several things that you may want to change in the default behavior of jQuery.Mobile. The easiest way to do this is to change the startup options. If you have created JavaScript with jQuery before, you are probably familiar with the `ready` event. In jQuery.Mobile, there is a similar event named `mobileinit` which is fired when the framework is loaded and before it renders the UI, so we can make changes here that will affect how the UI is created. One thing to note is that this needs to be included in your header BEFORE you include the **jQuery.Mobile.js** file, and AFTER you include the **jQuery.js** file, so your layout file should look like this:

```
<script src="http://code.jquery.com/jquery-1.6.4.min.js"
type="text/javascript"></script>
<script src="@Url.Content("~/Scripts/CustomJQMobileInit.js")"
   type="text/javascript"></script>
<script src="http://code.jquery.com/mobile/1.1.0/jquery.mobile-
1.1.0.min.js" type="text/javascript"></script>
```

So, what kinds of things would you want to change here? Let's suppose that we wanted to change the default page animation on every page from the default `"fade"` to `"flip"` because we like to see things flip. To do that, you would insert the following code in your **/Scripts/CustomJQMobileInit.js** file:

```
$(document).bind('mobileinit', function() {
   $.mobile.defaultPageTransition = "flip";
});
```

We could also use this if we had to create a multi-lingual site with localization. Some things like the text in the **Back** button are set by default within the framework. We can override this by setting one of the internal values in this initialization script.

There are also many other events that you should investigate such as the `pagebeforechange`, `pagebeforeload`, `pagebeforecreate`, `pagecreate`, `pageinit`, `pageload`, `pagebeforehide`, `pagebeforeshow`, `pagehide`, `pageshow`, and `pagechange`. All of these events in the jQuery.Mobile event model are available for you to access within JavaScript on your page.

There are too many details to go into here. There are several good jQuery.Mobile books that go into greater detail. This is just a quick introduction to give you a starting place for your research so that you know that it is possible to do these types of things with jQuery.Mobile.

Chapter 10   Enhancing Performance

"I feel the need...the need for speed!"
  Lt. Pete "Maverick" Mitchell in *Top Gun*

It's easy to say that we want a website that performs well. It's just as easy
to say that we've made changes and insist that our website is now "faster."
The real issue is how you can *measure* that performance increase. To show
that you have improved something, you first need to be able to measure it.
There are several ways that you can do that for a desktop application, but
not as many for mobile devices. However, there are a few options that work
fairly well for measuring performance on your mobile devices.

Measuring Performance

A great tool is one that many web developers are familiar with: YSlow. In addition to the normal desktop version that you can add as an extension to your browser, there is a mobile version available. This version is located at http://developer.yahoo.com/yslow/mobile. This URL will redirect you to a very long URL with lots of JavaScript on the end. To use YSlow for Mobile, you must first create a bookmark from this resulting URL, which will look like this:

```
http://yslow.org/mobile/#javascript:(function(y,p,o){p=y.body.append...
```

After you have created the bookmark, edit it and delete everything up to the "#" sign so that your bookmark is actually a piece of JavaScript code instead of a URL, which is commonly known as a bookmarklet. Once you have that bookmarklet, go back and load your site, click on the bookmarklet bookmark, and you should then see the YSlow application show up in the bottom half of your screen. It will reload the site and analyze it for you, giving you a score between 0 and 100, and a letter grade from A–F for both your overall site and each area.

Sometimes you can't do much about what it suggests. When analyzing an MVC site, it will suggest that the minified JavaScript and CSS should also be gzip compressed, but that option is not available in the MVC 4 RC bundles. As you review each area of your site, the tool will give you suggestions for how to improve your score in that area.

Enabling Client Caching with Web.config

One very easy way that you can dramatically speed up your website is to enable content caching on your scripts, style sheets, and images. To do that, all you need to do is to include this very simple **Web.config** in the **Content** and **Scripts** folders:

```xml
<?xml version="1.0" encoding="UTF-8"?>
<configuration>
  <system.webServer>
    <staticContent>
      <clientCache cacheControlMode="UseMaxAge"
        cacheControlMaxAge="30.00:00:00" />
    </staticContent>
  </system.webServer>
</configuration>
```

> Note that this is the Web.config in your subfolders, and not the Web.config in the root of your site!

You might not think you need this since your browser automatically caches images and other content files for you. However, if you look behind the scenes with a tool like Fiddler, you will see that even if your browser has a file in the cache, for each of the files on your page the browser will do an HTTP query up to the server to see if the file in the browser cache is older than the file on the server.

This Web.config setting will automatically put a content expiration date of thirty days on everything that is downloaded from that folder. The next time any of those images, scripts, or both are requested from that folder by your client's browser, it will see that it has the file in cache AND that the expiration date has not passed yet, so it won't hit the server to check and see if it needs the file. Even though it's a small request, you have eliminated one round-trip to the server for every image you have on the page that is cached. Talk about an easy upgrade!

There is one small downside to this approach that you have to be aware of. If you want to change a script, style sheet, or image in that folder, you have a small problem. For the next thirty days, any client that already has your script or image in its cache won't even bother to check your server to see if the file has changed. After thirty days, it will check again and your site will be updated.

Fortunately, there is a simple solution: When you change a file, you have to also change the name of the file. If you change a style sheet named **Site.Mobile.css**, do a global search and replace to change the name to **Site.Mobile2.css**. The new file name won't be in the client's cache, so it will be fetched from the server.

Using a CDN

Another way that you can easily increase the performance of your site is to use a content delivery network (CDN) for spreading the load for you. A CDN will dramatically improve your site's performance even if you are pulling the exact same files from the CDN that you serve up from your site. The secret is in how the browser retrieves files. Most browsers will download up to six concurrent files from any given domain. When you request a seventh resource from a domain, it will be queued up and wait until one of the first six are completed. If you download some of your files from a CDN, you get another six download streams that you can use at the same time.

Another big plus is that these files are cached in your browser's cache from some other site, so it's quite possible that they will already be there and you won't even have to download them.

You might think that you don't have access to one, but you do. You can easily use a CDN for the shared files that you include in your project. Here are some examples:

```
<link
href="http://code.jquery.com/mobile/1.1.0/jquery.mobile-1.1.0.min.css"
rel="stylesheet" />
<link
href="http://code.jquery.com/mobile/1.1.0/jquery.mobile.structure-
1.1.0.min.css" rel="stylesheet" />

<script
src="http://code.jquery.com/mobile/1.1.0/jquery.mobile-1.1.0.min.js"
type="text/javascript"></script>
<script src="http://code.jquery.com/jquery-1.6.4.min.js"
type="text/javascript"></script>
<script
src="http://ajax.aspnetcdn.com/ajax/mvc/3.0/jquery.unobtrusive-
ajax.min.js" type="text/javascript"></script>
<script
src="http://ajax.microsoft.com/ajax/jQuery.Validate/1.6/jQuery.Validate.min
type="text/javascript"></script>
<script
src="http://ajax.aspnetcdn.com/ajax/mvc/3.0/jquery.validate.unobtrusive.min
type="text/javascript"></script>
```

If you are using the bundling features of MVC 4, this may or may not apply to you, but it's worth looking at, at least for images that are not bundled and minified.

Data Prefetch Tag

On links that you know will be used (like a link to the next picture in a gallery), you can add an extra tag which will cause jQuery.Mobile to preload the content:

```
<a href="mypage" data-prefetch>Load Page</a>
```

The **data-prefetch** tag prompts jQuery.Mobile to go ahead and fetch the next page once the current page is loaded so that when you actually click on the link, the document will load almost instantaneously because the page is already in the cache.

In a similar fashion, jQuery.Mobile loads a page into memory in the DOM when it is loaded, and then removes the page when it goes out of scope, keeping up the three pages in memory at any given time. If you want to make sure your page remains in memory, you can add a **data-dom-cache="true"** on the page element, and it will not be unloaded, so it will load faster.

Both of these tips have a large potential downside if you are trying to manage page loads and memory yourself, so you will want to make sure it's important if you are planning on using these tips.

Chapter 11   Still Using MVC 3?

"I'll have what she's having!"
  Anonymous customer in *When Harry Met Sally*

There are a lot of projects out there that have been developed with MVC 3, and if you are still working with MVC 3, you may be feeling a little left out right now and want some of what everyone else is having. Don't worry about it—you can achieve the same mobile-friendly effects using existing MVC 3 technology, and position yourself to move right into MVC 4 without a big disruption.

Speed Bump: MVC 3 and MVC 4 side by side

You can easily install MVC 4 alongside MVC 3 and it is not *supposed* to break anything. However, there is one little speed bump that you may run into.

When MVC 4 is installed, it installs its new files for your system in the **C:\Program Files (x86)\Microsoft ASP.NET\ASP.NET MVC 4** folder, so it does keep the new MVC files separate from the ASP.NET MVC 3 folder that it sits beside. However, it also installs a new **v2.0** folder inside the **ASP.NET Web Pages** folder next to the **v1.0** folder: **C:\Program Files (x86)\Microsoft ASP.NET\ASP.NET Web Pages\v2.0**.

This folder just so happens to contain a few files that MVC 3 uses with the same name but a different version.

When you go back and build your existing MVC 3 project after installing MVC 4, you may get this compile error:

```
c:\Windows\Microsoft.NET\Framework\v4.0.30319\Microsoft.Common.targets(1360
warning MSB3247: Found conflicts between different versions of the same
dependent assembly.
```

If you dig around for a while, you'll find that your MVC 3 project references the **System.Web.Pages** and **System.Web.Helpers** DLLs, but without specifying a version. The quickest fix is to open up your project file in Notepad and make a couple of quick edits that put everything back in its proper place and your project will start working properly once again.

Project Definition File Before: (*.csproj)

```
<Reference Include="System.Web.WebPages">
  <Private>True</Private>
</Reference>
<Reference Include="System.Web.Helpers">
```

Project Definition File After: (*.csproj)

```
<Reference Include="System.Web.WebPages, Version=1.0.0.0, Culture=neutral,
  PublicKeyToken=31bf3856ad364e35, processorArchitecture=MSIL">
  <SpecificVersion>True</SpecificVersion>
</Reference>
<Reference Include="System.Web.Helpers, Version=1.0.0.0, Culture=neutral,
```

```
   PublicKeyToken=31bf3856ad364e35, processorArchitecture=MSIL">
     <Private>True</Private>
</Reference>
```

Once you've fixed that little bug, you should be able to run your MVC 3 projects normally again and everything works side by side. However, you will have to apply this fix to each and every MVC 3 project you open.

Back to the MVC 3 Project

Let's get back to our topic at hand: how do you convert your MVC 3 project to use the mobile-friendly techniques that we are using in our fancy new MVC 4 project? As it turns out, there is not much we need to add to make this work in MVC 3.

The first thing to do is to install the jQuery.Mobile package using NuGet, just like we do in MVC 4. Using the **Package Manager Console** command line, run the command **Install-Package jQuery.Mobile**.

Since the `DisplayModeProvider` code is a new feature in MVC 4, we will have to replicate that functionality in our MVC 3 project. In the root of your project, create a new class file called **MobileCapableRazorViewEngine.cs**, and put the following code into that class:

```csharp
using System;
using System.IO;
using System.Web;
using System.Web.Mvc;

namespace YourApplicationNameSpace
{
  // In Global.asax.cs Application_Start you can insert these
  // into the ViewEngine chain like so:
  //
  // ViewEngines.Engines.Insert(0, new
  //   MobileCapableRazorViewEngine());
  //
  // or
  //
  // ViewEngines.Engines.Insert(0,
  //   new MobileCapableRazorViewEngine("iPhone")
  //   {
  //     ContextCondition = (ctx =>
  //       ctx.Request.UserAgent.IndexOf(
  //         "iPhone", StringComparison.OrdinalIgnoreCase) >= 0)
  //   });

  public class MobileCapableRazorViewEngine : RazorViewEngine
  {
    public string ViewModifier { get; set; }
    public Func<HttpContextBase, bool> ContextCondition
      { get; set; }

    public MobileCapableRazorViewEngine()
      : this("Mobile", context =>
        context.Request.Browser.IsMobileDevice)
    {
    }
```

```csharp
public MobileCapableRazorViewEngine(string viewModifier)
  : this(viewModifier,
    context => context.Request.Browser.IsMobileDevice)
{
}

public MobileCapableRazorViewEngine(string viewModifier,
  Func<HttpContextBase, bool> contextCondition)
{
  this.ViewModifier = viewModifier;
  this.ContextCondition = contextCondition;
}

public override ViewEngineResult FindView(
 ControllerContext controllerContext,
 string viewName, string masterName, bool useCache)
{
  return NewFindView(controllerContext, viewName,
    null, useCache, false);
}

public override ViewEngineResult FindPartialView(
  ControllerContext controllerContext,
  string partialViewName, bool useCache)
{
  return NewFindView(controllerContext, partialViewName,
    null, useCache, true);
}

private ViewEngineResult NewFindView(
  ControllerContext controllerContext,
  string viewName, string masterName, bool useCache,
  bool isPartialView)
{
  if (!ContextCondition(controllerContext.HttpContext))
  {
    // We found nothing and we pretend we looked nowhere.
    return new ViewEngineResult(new string[] { });
  }

  // Get the name of the controller from the path.
  string controller = controllerContext.RouteData
    .Values["controller"].ToString();
  string area = "";
  try
  {
    area = controllerContext.RouteData.DataTokens["area"]
    .ToString();
  }
  catch
  {
  }

  // Apply the view modifier.
  var newViewName = string.Format("{0}.{1}", viewName,
    ViewModifier);

  // Create the key for caching purposes.
```

```csharp
string keyPath = Path.Combine(area, controller,
  newViewName);

string cacheLocation =
  ViewLocationCache
    .GetViewLocation(controllerContext.HttpContext,
    keyPath);

// Try the cache.
if (useCache)
{
  //If using the cache, check to see if the location
  //is cached.
  if (!string.IsNullOrWhiteSpace(cacheLocation))
  {
    if (isPartialView)
    {
      return new ViewEngineResult(CreatePartialView(
        controllerContext, cacheLocation), this);
    }
    else
    {
      return new ViewEngineResult(
        CreateView(controllerContext, cacheLocation,
        masterName),
          this);
    }
  }
}
string[] locationFormats = string.IsNullOrEmpty(area) ?
  ViewLocationFormats : AreaViewLocationFormats;

// For each of the paths defined, format the string and
// see if that path exists. When found, cache it.
foreach (string rootPath in locationFormats)
{
  string currentPath = string.IsNullOrEmpty(area)
    ? string.Format(rootPath, newViewName, controller)
    : string.Format(rootPath, newViewName, controller,
      area);
  if (FileExists(controllerContext, currentPath))
  {
    ViewLocationCache.InsertViewLocation(
      controllerContext.HttpContext,
      keyPath, currentPath);
    if (isPartialView)
    {
      return new ViewEngineResult(CreatePartialView(
        controllerContext, currentPath), this);
    }
    else
    {
      return new ViewEngineResult(CreateView(
        controllerContext, currentPath, masterName),
          this);
    }
  }
}
```

```
      // We found nothing and we pretend we looked nowhere.
      return new ViewEngineResult(new string[] { });
    }
  }
}
```

This code is also available on NuGet by running the following command:

```
PM> Install-Package MobileViewEngines
```

If you install the NuGet package, it won't automatically include the code in your project, but the code will be in the **Packages** folder alongside your project, so you can copy it from there.

> Kudos for this code go to Scott Hanselman, who blogged about this mobile view approach[5], and Peter Mourfield, who contributed this version of the Mobile View Engine code!

Now that you have the view engine available for use, edit the **Global.asax.cs** file and update the `Application_Start` function with the following code (which looks amazingly similar to what we did for MVC 4!):

```
protected void Application_Start()
{
  AreaRegistration.RegisterAllAreas();
  RegisterGlobalFilters(GlobalFilters.Filters);
  RegisterRoutes(RouteTable.Routes);

  ViewEngines.Engines.Insert(0,
  new MobileCapableRazorViewEngine("Phone")
  {
    ContextCondition = (ctx =>
      ctx.Request.UserAgent.IndexOf("iPhone",
        StringComparison.OrdinalIgnoreCase) >= 0 ||
      ctx.Request.UserAgent.IndexOf("iPod",
        StringComparison.OrdinalIgnoreCase) >= 0 ||
      ctx.Request.UserAgent.IndexOf("Droid",
        StringComparison.OrdinalIgnoreCase) >= 0 ||
      ctx.Request.UserAgent.IndexOf("Blackberry",
        StringComparison.OrdinalIgnoreCase) >= 0 ||
      ctx.Request.UserAgent.StartsWith("Blackberry",
        StringComparison.OrdinalIgnoreCase))
  });
  ViewEngines.Engines.Insert(0,
  new MobileCapableRazorViewEngine("Tablet")
  {
    ContextCondition = (ctx =>
      ctx.Request.UserAgent.IndexOf("iPad",
        StringComparison.OrdinalIgnoreCase) >= 0 ||
      ctx.Request.UserAgent.IndexOf("Playbook",
        StringComparison.OrdinalIgnoreCase) >= 0 ||
```

```
    ctx.Request.UserAgent.IndexOf("Transformer",
        StringComparison.OrdinalIgnoreCase) >= 0 ||
    ctx.Request.UserAgent.IndexOf("Xoom",
        StringComparison.OrdinalIgnoreCase) >= 0)
  });
}
```

That's it—you now have a code base that is almost functionally equivalent to what we have created using the MVC 4 mobile functionality with the **DisplayModeProvider**. There are a few differences, but you should be able to start creating a very mobile-friendly website using this code base. The jQuery.Mobile features should all be the same, and most of the layout files should be the same. There are a few things like the bundling technology that are not available in MVC 3, so you will have to list each of your style sheets and JavaScript files in your layout files (or minify and concatenate them yourself).

The following figure is an example of an MVC 3 application with a screenshot of the code for the layout page, a screenshot of the resulting familiar, blue, tabbed, default layout for the desktop, and the updated phone layout with the title changed to **Phone Home Page**.

MVC 3 App with Desktop and Phone Layouts

When you combine this technique with the things you learned about earlier in the book, you should be able to start making your MVC 3 applications nearly as mobile-friendly as MVC 4 applications!

Chapter 12   Conclusion

"No more training do you require. Already know you that which you need."
  Yoda in *Star Wars Episode VI: Return of the Jedi*

Creating mobile-friendly websites is not difficult to do if you know how. It's something you CAN do, and it's something you SHOULD start doing right now. If you don't have one, I would encourage you to get a mobile device and experiment with your current websites and see how they look. Making a few of the simple changes in this book can greatly improve your site and make you look like a rock star.

I hope you've enjoyed this book and that you've learned something. I know that I've learned a lot doing the research for this book and discovering new things about topics that I *thought* I already knew.

So what are you waiting for? Go forth and create mobile-friendly websites!

And while you're at it, go learn something new today!